MW01611122

I AM RAMLA

Ramla Tarkhani-Lloyd

Copyright © 2020 Ramla Tarkhani-Lloyd

Some names have been changed to protect the privacy of certain individuals.

No part of this publication may be reproduced, stored in a retrieval system, or transmitted in any way, by any means, whether electronically, mechanically, via photocopy, recording, or otherwise without the prior written permission of the publisher except as provided by USA copyright law.

Publishing assistance provided by TJS Publishing House
www.tjspublishinghouse.com
IG: @ tjspublishinghouse
FB: @ tjspublishinghouse
tjspublishinghouse@gmail.com

Cover design by TJS Publishing House

Published in the United States of America
Paperback ISBN-13: 978-0-578-64827-9
Paperback ISBN-10: 0-578-64827-X

DEDICATION

The time is finally here, the true story about my childhood is finished, and I'm dedicating this book to my kids, my three boys.

INTRODUCTION

It was very hard to start, continue, and finish writing this book. It took me over 13 years to really be at peace with myself and complete it. I took breaks for years, working up the courage and fighting through lots of tears to get back at it, and finally, to finish it.

Writing this book woke up all of the good and bad memories and thoughts I had from this period of my life. I began feeling the same pain all over again. There was not one day I wouldn't feel broken or cry when I read my life story. It always felt like someone was choking me while I was working on this book. The pain is still so deep that it affects me to this day.

I had times where I felt like giving up on it because I believed I would never finish my story. But something inside always convinced me to go back to it. I felt that everything that happened to me needed to be shared. I hope it will help you or anyone who will face or has faced situations like I have. I hope my story will help you learn from my experiences and avoid wasting precious time with the wrong person.

Welcome to my life. It's a true, sad, fun, adventurous, yet beautiful story. I hope you will enjoy this crazy rollercoaster ride, and please DO NOT JUDGE.

Enjoy the wild ride, which is my life.

CONTENTS

ACKNOWLEDGMENTS

I would like to express my special thanks of gratitude to God, my husband, teachers, dance teacher (RIP), neighbors, my first son who changed me drastically, and everyone else who tried to put their lives on the line to help me out of my dangerous situations. I am really thankful to them.

Secondly, I would like to thank my parents (RIP Dad). You made me who I am today, and I know that it was all love, and you just wanted the best for me. That was your way to show it. I will never say what you did to me was ok, but I understand why you were who you were. I miss you, and I love you, and I hope you rest in peace. Mom, thank you for your patience with Dad and with me. Words can't describe how much I love you.

Thanks to all my friends who helped me a lot in finalizing this project within this very long timeframe.

I thank everyone who was a part of my book, whether it was a good or a bad experience. I learned through those emotions, and God sent all of those people to me for a reason.

I thank God so much for always helping me out when I get into a dangerous moment, for protecting me from the devil who is always trying to stir things up in my life, and for all those beautiful angels you sent when things got hot. Sometimes I can smell those angels around me. God is always there for me when I did the wrong thing, and only He knows what I have been through.

It's God that I give all honor to.

CHAPTER 1
INNOCENT SOUL

Ramla, age 10.

Hey, my name is Ramla. I am ten years old. I was born and raised in Hamburg, Germany, in a crazy town called Jenfeld. It is a very dangerous neighborhood. There are lots of drugs, robbery, and crime. There are many poor to middle-class people living there.

I hate my first name, "Ramla"! "Ramla" is an Arabic name that means "sand grain". "Sand grain" is a beautiful thing if you live in that country, but in Germany, "Ramla" means something totally different. Just so you know, the name "RAMLER" (which sounds so close to "Ramla") is the male version of a rabbit who loves to have sex 24/7. As a little girl, I do not want to be affiliated with any of that, even when I grow up.

Kids laugh and bully me every single day. I am

embarrassed all the time! When someone asks my name, whether at the doctor's office, on the streets, in school, or wherever, I feel so humiliated. I get harassed a lot because of my name, in and outside of school. I can't believe my parents gave me that name!!!

I need to do something about the bullying. It is so bad that I'm changing my own first name as soon as possible. I'm going with the name "Kim". Everyone that I meet from now on and even all my old friends need to call me Kim. Why Kim? No reason at all. It was the first name that popped into my mind. I can't take the name "Ramla" anymore!!

Ramla, present day.

We were going on a road trip from Germany to Italy. From there, we'd take the cruise to Tunisia, North Africa, where my parents are from. I couldn't wait!

My dad always planned all the vacation details. He made sure his van was on point. Sandwiches were made, the cooler was packed with drinks, and we were ready to go. I'd packed my suitcase weeks in advance, and I was so excited that I couldn't fall asleep that night. I told myself that the swaying of the car would eventually rock me to sleep when we got onto the road.

What an awesome time we had! It was a wonderful summer. Just me, my dad, my mom, my little brother, and my little sister. I was probably 10 years old at the time. My dad and I were very close. I was his little girl, his little princess. I can't even remember having any issues with my father back then.

Twenty-four hours passed by, and we made it to Sicily Italy, all the way from Germany. I remember the wonderfully hot summer weather of the beautiful city. I also remember that we got lost in Sicily. We looked for the port, but since none of us knew Italian or English, we almost missed our cruise! But with my mom's help and her common sense, we made it to the port. The gigantic cruise ship was waiting for us, and they let us park our van in the belly of the giant boat. Up we went to our cabin to rest because we had another long 24 hours of travel to go until we reached North Africa.

Back in the day, it was exciting to go to Tunisia. It was a paradise on earth with clear water, clean sand, and no danger in sight. But today, after the revolution, that beautiful Tunisia is just a memory. Now, you can get robbed or killed easily. It's just not the same anymore. I can't wait for the day to call Tunisia paradise again.

My beautiful mother is from the city, and my dad is from the suburbs. I never knew that this could eventually be a problem one day in a relationship or marriage, especially when you dearly love the city. Being married now, I learned it can be a huge problem.

In Tunisia, we were traveling between my mom's family, who lived in the city by the beach, and my father's house, which was far away, by the mountains. Except for my father, we all hated to visit his home in the mountains. It was so boring! There was absolutely nothing for us to do over there except hang out in my dad's huge mansion in the middle of nowhere.

I adored my mom's side of the family. I always felt the love. It was so real. Also, I will never forget how my grandfather, Baba Lachthir (RIP), used to stay up all night to take care of me when I had asthma attacks. It was awful! I couldn't breathe normally, so breathing at all was very hard. I always had to have an asthma pump.

While everyone was asleep at night, my cough got worse. I was up all night, coughing and spitting out mucus that was stuck in my chest. My grandfather used to hold my head with one hand and held an empty bean can in his other hand so I could spit the mucus into it. I know it sounds gross, but that's how

I knew that man loved me.

I was limited in so many things because of my asthma. I couldn't run for a full minute or even walk upstairs without having trouble. My breathing would bother me right away.

I remember the trip we made from my mom's family to my dad's house like it was yesterday. We'd been driving, and after about an hour, my dad pulled our car onto an empty road. Even though it was nighttime and dark, I could see a huge beautiful mountain and a house near the top of it. The house had lights on, and it looked like a shining star sitting on top of the mountain. My dad told me to get out while my mom and siblings stayed in the car.

"We have to climb that mountain to see a healing lady. She is the best, and she will heal you. Today is your last day of asthma," he said to me. I didn't believe him, but at this point, I was ready to try anything! I wanted to breathe, sleep, run, walk fast, and play in gym class normally like everyone else back in Germany.

I took his hand, and we started to climb the mountain. It was actually very easy to climb. I had no breathing problems. When we finally reached the top, I saw a line of people in front of her house, which turned out to be more like a tent.

"Do you see all those people? Each one of them is sick with whatever disease. They are all here to see this old lady. She is a gift from God. She will heal all of them." My dad skipped everyone in line and told me it was okay because I was a child. Her rule was, kids went first.

I was first in line, almost inside her tent. Then I saw her coming. She was so short, maybe four feet tall. She had fiery red hair and was cute. She came outside, took my hand, and walked me away from all those people. My dad never left my side.

"Open your mouth," she said.

I opened, and she put her hand inside my mouth, and then almost her entire arm. I was so uncomfortable. It didn't hurt, but it felt like she was scratching the slimy mucus out of me from the inside. Then she removed her arm. I fell on my knees and began to throw up. The more I vomited, the better I felt. All of the vomit was mucus that had made me miserable for so long. After I finished vomiting, I got up, and I felt like a newborn baby. My asthma was gone that day, forever! No more doctor visits, shots, or pump. I was HEALED!

She didn't charge my father anything, but he gave her a little gift, and we left.

"Wow, what a blessing this lady is!" I told my dad.

"Yes, she is. A real healer never asks for money. They do it because that's their purpose in life."

If someone had told me this story, I would have thought they were telling me a fairy tale, but this actually happened to me. So whatever story I hear about healers, especially from AFRICA, I have believed from that day forward.

I remember one sunny afternoon at my dad's place, I was so bored staring at nothing on the balcony. I started biting on my knee. I still have the bite mark on my right knee today. I was ten years old.

I heard the doorbell ringing. It was my father's neighbor and friend. He asked my father if I wanted to go to an outdoor wedding event with him. My dad had told him I was dying of boredom, so I guess this was his way of providing a way to get me out of the house.

My dad said, "Come on. Get out of the house and have some fun. You are going with my friend, our neighbor across the street, to an event."

I was so excited that I didn't even change my clothes! I remember exactly what I was wearing that day and how I had my hair styled. I left with my Capri Jeans, my baby blue Mickey Mouse T-shirt, and my pigtails. All I was thinking was, *Just get me out of this house, please!*

My dad's friend and I were walking to the event. It wasn't that far from our house. While we were walking, about 10 minutes later, he put his arm around me.

Ok...That was awkward. But I thought, *What can he do? It's my dad's friend, right?* His arm started going down my chest, and he was rubbing on my breast. *Like, really?* I was very young, and I was just starting to develop. When he started to feel on me, I told myself, *I am 10 years old, and not dumb years old.* I knew that this touching was wrong, and I just wanted to go back home, but I didn't have the courage to say it to him. I stayed with him at the event. It felt like forever. Thank God he didn't try more or anything else. He dropped me back home, and I was disturbed about it for the entire summer.

I never said a word to my parents. I felt dirty and blamed myself. Why? I don't know why. If my dad ever found out, he would have probably killed that guy and buried him in our backyard. So, I just kept that to myself and saved his friend's life.

That whole trip was a mess. After that incident, all I wanted was to go home. I was so happy when our vacation was over, and we landed back in Germany.

CHAPTER 2
THE CRUSH

Five years passed, and I became an emotional fifteen-year-old teenage girl. My first love, my first boyfriend, was a crazy white boy who was my first everything. When I say white boy, I mean his eyebrows and eyelashes were platinum blonde. That's how he got the nickname, Blondy. Every girl wanted to be with him, and every boy in town wanted to be him. He was very charming, and he had that special something.

Blondy was the next-door neighbor of my best friend, Brittney. Blondy was dating a beautiful dark-haired, tall Persian girl when I met him. I was definitely turned off from the fact that he was taken, but I knew how to back off and let go of my feelings. Very funny to hear that from a teenage girl, right? When he came over to my best friend's house, the more I saw him, the more I talked to him, the more I wanted him! At the same time, I admired his relationship with his Persian beauty too. I'm a firm believer in karma (what goes around comes back around), so I didn't try to pursue him at all. I didn't want any girl to take my man away from me one day.

It was 1993 in Hamburg, Germany. My father was disciplined. I had a very strict father–over the top strict–especially when it came to boys. My father was the type of person who was unforgiving. The type that if you made one little mistake, he would beat you into a coma, and it didn't matter if you were a grown-up or child, a man or a woman. But with me, he was always cool. I was his little girl. I remember at that time I thought I had the best family ever. That is until the most unexpected day of my life came. But before I talk about that, we have to go back to Blondy again.

It was a regular summer high school day. All of the students were on a lunch break. I was hanging out in the schoolyard with my two best friends, Brittney and Jenny. We were about to walk back to our classroom when we passed by Blondy's girlfriend, the Persian beauty. When I looked up to her, I noticed she had a black eye. Everyone in the entire town was talking about a girl who got beat up by her boyfriend for trying to end the relationship. Now I knew what couple everyone was gossiping about. It was Blondy and his Persian girlfriend. I was totally in shock, but when I saw her black eye, I was just speechless.

Blondy had beaten her badly because she wanted to break up with him (for whatever reason). *Like What??? Is this guy serious??? Is this the same guy I fell for???* I thought. I was so surprised. I thought he was the man! Believe it or not, even though I heard about all of the drama between him and her, and I saw her beaten up face with my own eyes, I wanted him more than ever. What was wrong with me??? It was just a matter of time until I heard Blondy and his Persian girl broke up for good.

As I'm writing this portion of my book, I realize how sick it sounds, but that's the extreme in me. I'm a good girl with an extraordinary mind. I see the beauty in everyone, even in the wrong ones, and I always feel like I can change a lousy human being into a good one.

An entire year had passed, and summer break was back again. Like every summer, my dad used to take us to our home country, Tunisia. I used to stay there for the entire summer break, which was about two months. While I was in Tunisia, I decided to have a total makeover and transform from a tomboy into a girly-girl. So, when I got back to Germany after two months of vacation, I felt like a new person with much more confidence. No one could stop the happiness I had.

A couple of days passed by, and I bumped into Blondy. I knew it was just a matter of time until I would. I was in front of my building, talking to my best friend Brittney and boom! He came from out of nowhere and was standing very close behind me.

"I love your tan, Ramla. You look so beautiful. Where did you go? I didn't see you for a while," he said.

Oh my God, I thought as my heart dropped. *Did he just notice me? Did he just say what he said? Is he flirting with me?*

I was shocked and had butterflies in my stomach. I couldn't speak! The most important thing is that I totally forgot about what he'd done to the Persian beauty a year ago.

I started to have a conversation with him and tried not to show how I felt about him. After our small talk, he walked away, but then he turned back around and asked me if I want to hang out with him the next day. That was the beginning of a horrible time in my life. That was the push of the first domino in a series of terrible events in my life.

The first couple of months were beautiful. We were both so in love with each other. He was actually more in love with me than I was with him. He was obsessed with me. However, our love story did not last for long.

After just eight months of dating, reality kicked me in my face, and the most terrifying part of my life started. Blondy turned into a psychopath. He began to get jealous of everyone all of a sudden, and no one, not even people who said good morning to me, was safe. I couldn't even hang out with my best friends anymore. I couldn't walk on the streets without him starting trouble with people who looked my way.

He was so possessive over me that I started to feel uncomfortable. We reached a point where his behavior wasn't funny or sexy anymore. It was just a lot of stress. Hello! I'm only 16 years old, dealing with all that drama. Should I be stressed out at that age? I really don't think so.

I remember one day, my girlfriend Nicole was over my house while my parents were at work. He called my house phone and asked me who was in my house. I told him my classmate was there. Five minutes later, he knocked on my door and went after my friend! Blondy dragged her out of my apartment to the hallway and started to beat her.

Ok, so how can I get rid of this guy now?

I tried to help my friend. There was a moment where I was holding him, and she was able to run out of the building, but he continued to chase her. I remember she had no shoes on when she ran out, and when he caught her, he continued to beat her.

I wasn't so attracted to him anymore. I fell in love with charming Blondy, not insecure, violent Blondy. It was insane and unhealthy.

I couldn't believe what had happened. Thank God my father wasn't home! My parents were usually at work Monday through Friday, from 5 pm to 8 pm. If I had friends over, I tried to bring them to my house between those hours. I did all that sneaking around because my father didn't let me do shit back then. The more he said I couldn't do something, the more I did it.

After all of that craziness was over, I went downstairs to the parking lot, where I'd decided to tell him I was done with him. I didn't think anything of it when I said it. I just knew hitting my classmate was too much for me, and all I wanted was for the relationship to be over.

I told him that I wasn't looking for a partner who is violent to me, to my people, or to anybody else.

He looked at me and said, "You're never going to leave me." Then he started to attack me. It was broad daylight. He beat me up in that parking lot, and no one on the streets offered to help! I remember I was on the ground, and he was kicking me in my stomach. He only stopped when I said that I'd changed my mind and was not going to leave him.

That was actually the second time he'd hit me. I tried to end it with him a few weeks before at his house. He started to hit me like a crazy maniac until I couldn't take it anymore. So, I lied and told him I would never leave him, so he would stop beating me.

I told myself that this time was the last time he would put his hands on me. I was so scared of Blondy. I knew if I tried to break up with him, I would get beaten up again. And who was going to help me? Everyone was scared of him because nobody wanted any problems with Blondy. I couldn't tell my father about him, because I was hiding this relationship from him, so I'd not get beat up by my father. How bizarre is all that, right?

Everyone in the neighborhood heard the rumors about me dating Blondy. Every family in town knew that he was abusing me. I mean, everyone! My mom, brother, teachers, and neighbors knew. Everyone knew except for one person–my father. My father had no clue that I was dating, much less that I was going through all this trauma.

CHAPTER 3
THE BREAKUP

I never thought the day would come when my dad would find out that I had a boyfriend. Unfortunately, my boyfriend Blondy was a psycho. It was just a matter of time until the bomb exploded.

It was a sunny afternoon. My parents had gone to work. My brother Ferris was hanging outside with his friends, and I was babysitting my little sister Bella like always.

I'd broken up with Blondy again. I thought, *Wow, maybe he will get it this time and leave me alone.* As soon as I thought that, he was knocking at my door. I did not open it even though he was knocking and knocking. Then his knocking turned into banging and boom! The door was on the floor. He had kicked our front door open!

He came in and destroyed our apartment. He destroyed our entire home. Chandeliers were ripped out the ceiling and lamps lay broken in pieces on the floor. He even broke our bathtub in half! The door wasn't there anymore. Everyone was able just to walk in. It looked like someone threw a bomb into our apartment.

There was nothing I could do to stop him. All I was thinking was that I would be a dead girl in a few minutes when my dad came home. How could I explain this to my father? What kind of person destroys things like that? His actions showed me again that this boy was mentally ill. He made all that mess and then left.

I was so scared!! I didn't know what I'd say to my father. I remember trying to figure out the most believable lie.

Think, think, think faster, the clock is ticking! He can't find out that I have a psycho boyfriend. He can't even find out that I have a boyfriend at all! I'm a Muslim! I'm not supposed to have a boyfriend until I get married!! I know my father's pride is going to be so hurt if he ever finds out, especially since he is the number one psycho.

Everybody knew my father or had heard about him. My father was very respected by everyone in our community, including police officers. No one wanted to fuck with him—ever. Let's just say it like that.

In a few minutes, my parents would be home from work. I was done. I just knew I was dead. My mom walked in first, and her mouth was wide open in shock.

"What the hell happened in here?"

"Mom, I'm so sorry! I really tried to break up with him, but he just won't leave me alone! I don't know what to do. This is the result of me trying to leave him."

My mother was not that strict, and she knew about Blondy, but she also warned me about him. She knew that he wasn't any good for me because he started lots of unnecessary drama, but she'd also heard about his abusive past with the Persian girl. When she walked into the house and saw all that mess, I knew she was fed up with everything.

"You need to tell your father. Otherwise, I'll tell him."

Wait. What?? Tell my father? Is she out of her mind? He will kill me! This is not a father where you just sit down and have small talk about your boyfriend, and everything is beautiful after.

This is a father who doesn't care about anyone except himself and his respected name. Of course, he loved us, but only if we walked in his lane.

Everyone who takes a shortcut was dead to him.

He kept guns in the house. He had got a gun for every occasion. I was scared of him. I did not want him to know about this.

I was begging my mom, "Please don't tell him!" I started shaking and crying.

"Ok, this is the last time I will cover for you, but you better believe this is the LAST time."

My dad walked in. He stood there, looking around at the mess. He looked at my mom.

"Who did all this?"

My mom told him that I did it. She wanted to play the   "Oh-my-God-our-daughter–is-mentally-not-right" role.

"It was Ramla, your daughter. I think that Ramla had her five minutes. I think she is going crazy." The straight poker face my mom had was priceless. All that to protect me from my father.

My dad's expression was like a huge question mark. You could see his wheels turning and him thinking, *Where did Ramla get the strength to break the bathtub in half?* He just acted as if he believed my mom and started to fix the door. My father was quiet all night. I felt so bad for doing this to him.

We never ever talked about what happened that day again.

After the chaos in my apartment, my father started to do a little research. All that drama was too much for him. Neighbors started talking and telling my dad stories of what had been happening to me. Blondy was mentioned, and especially the fact that he was hitting me. My father never questioned me about the rumors. He was just ready to catch me in my lies.

I started to smoke a lot of weed, and I was high all the time. At least when I was high, I was able to deal with Blondy. One day I was hanging out at Blondy's house, and I was super high from smoking weed. After a while, I realized that I had to leave so I could get home before my dad did. I wasn't too concerned because it always worked out for me. Well, except for this particular day.

I walked down the stairs. I remember I had a skirt, a tank top, and high heels on. So, when I opened the door to leave the building, there he was. My dad. He was standing with his back to me. My reaction was lightning fast. I backed up slowly, closed the door, and ran back inside the building.

I ran back to Blondy's third-floor apartment. When I reached his door, I banged on it like a crazy person. He opened the door.

"What happened?"

"Give me a sheet, a rope, or something. Anything. I have to slide down your balcony right now. I need to get home before my dad does." Even though the situation was serious, I said this to him like it wasn't a big deal. He looked at me like I was crazy, but to me, the risk of jumping was so much less than getting caught at Blondy's house. *Let's do this! It doesn't even matter if I die trying to make this jump. I would rather die trying than face him about Blondy!*

Blondy looked at me and said, "Are you completely crazy now? I live on the third floor! You know that, right? That's really dangerous! You can die!" But I screamed at him so loud that he knew without a doubt that I was ready to jump. He saw it in my eyes.

I asked him again, "Bring me a rope or something so I can slide down it!"

He went to his room to look, but when he came back, I had already jumped. Yes, I jumped down the third story building with my high heels on. I landed on my back. I looked up, and I saw Blondy on his balcony looking down.

"Oh my God! Are you ok? Are you ok? Are you in pain?" he asked.

At that moment, I didn't hear or see anyone clearly. All I knew was I needed to get up and go home. NOW. I do remember that as I was landing, I saw two little kids playing on the second-floor balcony, and they called their dad.

"Daddy! Daddy!! A big bird just fell from the sky!"

Their dad looked at me and asked me why didn't I jump off the roof? *What an idiot,* I thought. All I was thinking at that point was to get up and make it home before my dad got back to the house.

I COULDN'T FEEL ANYTHING.

CHAPTER 4
DADDY'S LITTLE GIRL

It's crazy how you can be so scared of someone that it will give you adrenaline. I got up and began to walk home. There was a tunnel where you can walk through to get to my building. When I entered that tunnel, to my surprise, my dad entered the tunnel at the same time from the opposite end, and we ended up meeting in the middle. I remember thinking, *Why did I even jump? He got me anyway. I will die today.* He took my hand and walked home with me with a sneaky smile on his face. He wanted to show the neighbors who were standing outside that everything was fine.

As soon as we walked into our building and got inside the elevator, he started to beat me. He didn't even ask me any questions. He just went crazy. He took my head and smashed it against the elevator wall. I can't even tell you how many times or how long he did that. I guess as long as it takes from the ground floor to the third floor in a slow-moving elevator. I just know it felt forever. When I came out of the elevator, I had a huge bump on my forehead and a black, blue, and purple eye. I was bleeding so much that my clothes were drenched with blood, and my bottom lip was bleeding, cracked, and swollen.

As we walked into our apartment, he continued to beat me up. I remember I was lying on my back on the floor while he was on top of me, punching and beating me up. Then he got up, grabbed our heavy TV, and threw it on my stomach. I guess that was the end of that. Until today, I don't know how I survived.

No one deserves to get beaten up like that! He beat me up like I was some dude on the street. He was a strong man, and I was a little girl. I couldn't defend myself even if I tried. He used his bare fist to hit me (not even a slap or a smack). His *FIST*.

He told me to go to my room. I was grounded. He explained there would be no school for me, at least for the next couple of weeks, until my face and bruises healed. Of course, I couldn't go anywhere the way I looked. My face was smashed like a mashed potato! If anyone saw me like that, especially my teachers, they would take me away from home.

My mother and siblings were in shock when they saw me. My brother was too young to fight Blondy, so he decided to run to his house and tell Blondy everything was his fault. My brother never forgot what happened to me, even to this day.

My mom started a huge argument with my dad, but he couldn't care less what my mother had to say; it was always his way or the highway. My mother was pretty much helpless because she was so dependent on my father. She couldn't just get up and leave him. One reason was she didn't speak German. Also, she didn't have any family or friends in Germany. So she was stuck with him. She felt like there was no way out, and only God could help at that point.

My father never hit me when my mother was around. He told her whatever he could to keep her calm. Especially when he did something to one of us that she wouldn't approve of. He did this all the time. I couldn't believe how my mom could always believe him when all along he was the one beating my brother and me up. She always fell for his lies. But this time was different. This time, my bruises spoke for themselves, so once she saw them, she believed me. She finally saw for herself that my father was a MONSTER and that he was beating up her children while she was at work.

I always told myself I never wanted to end up like my mother and be with a man like my father. Why is she so naive? Why is she not doing anything about it? When I asked her those questions, she said she was very scared of him, and if she ever left him, he would kill her. I remember holding her hands, looking deep into her eyes, and telling her we should run away together. I spoke fluent German, and we could do it. But she was too scared of him. She thought he would really kill her if she left him.

My father always walked around with a gun, and he didn't care about anything. He didn't fear anyone, except God. I remember he always said he would not care about going to jail. He had no issue with killing someone who disrespected him. He meant that to his core.

I will never forget how my father woke me up the day after he almost killed me in the elevator. All I felt was ice cold water on my head. I jumped out of bed, confused about what had just happened. Imagine someone waking you up like that. It's freaking crazy! My father lost his mind like that just because I had a boyfriend??? The worst thing was, he was upset about a boyfriend that I did not want anymore who I was trying to get rid of!

When he woke me up like that, I knew that was his way of saying he wasn't done with me. My mother was already at work, and my brother was at school. The only person who was home with me was my little sister, Bella, who was only six years old at the time. Unfortunately for her, she saw everything that happened, but she couldn't do a thing to help.

I was standing in the room with my hair, face, and pajamas soaking wet. He called me to the dining room and told me to take a seat. He'd set up his barber chair in the dining room and waited for me to sit on it. I knew what was about to happen, but I thought for a moment I was overreacting. I soon discovered I wasn't. He completely chopped off all my long, spiral, ruby red curls.

All of that happened right in front of my little sister. She was in her thirties when I wrote this book, and she told me she would never forget that day. Every single detail of it is stuck with her for life.

I looked in the mirror, and I couldn't believe what he had done. I had this weird, short looking haircut. Not to mention, my face still looked like a truck had run over it from where he'd punched me in the elevator. I had a black eye, and my bottom lip was swollen. The huge cartoon-like knot was on my forehead. I cried for days, and I even thought of taking my life. But to be honest, I was too chicken and I would never do that. I believe in God and I always thought everything happened for a reason. I also believed it couldn't get worse than it already was.

Probably a week went by, and I was still grounded. No school, no friends, no nothing. It was just another day with my dad and me at home. I was missing a lot of days of school. It was my last year in high school, and I needed to be in school to graduate with my class. My days of having perfect attendance were over, and my record of having good grades, and good relationships with the people at my school was on hold. I know they were wondering what was going on. I wouldn't have been able to focus at school with all the stress going on at home anyway.

On this particular day, I was in my room performing in front of my mirror, like always, dreaming about being a big superstar someday. Then I heard someone knocking on our front door. I stayed in my room, listening to see who it was. It was Blondy. I remembered how my brother had run to him before and told him that everything was his fault and that my dad had beaten me up badly. I guess Blondy had decided to come to my father and thought he could tell him how bad of a father he was. I remember thinking I hoped he'd signed his funeral papers because it was about to go down.

I never left my room. I was too scared of my father,

and I knew my dad had this situation handled. All I heard was consistent hard punching and Blondy screaming at the top of his lungs for help. I actually had mixed feelings at this point. First, I was thinking, *Finally, someone is beating the dude up who has been beating me up! What now? How about you try to hit my father now, Blondy? Oh, it's not the same as when you hit me, right, Blondy?*

My father had never met Blondy before, so he didn't know what he looked like. In the midst of the fight, my father put two and two together and knew right away that this was the guy that his daughter was dealing with, and this was the guy who had destroyed our home. He knew that this was the guy who put his hands on his daughter multiple times before, and on top of that, this guy had the nerve to come and knock at his door to tell him what a bad father he was?

In fact, Blondy was very lucky it turned out that well. When my father opened the door, he had only a towel around him, because he'd just come out of the shower. I overheard my father telling my mother that while he was beating up Blondy, he lost the towel, and that's how Blondy had the chance to run for his life. If not, my dad would have probably killed him.

My father let so much anger out on Blondy that

Blondy lost the vision in one eye. My father ended up paying monthly payments by court order for years for the damage to Blondy's eye, but my father never cared about that. He always used to say that he'd rather pay the price rather than having a wannabe gangster messing with his pride. The next day, I asked my mom to let me see Blondy and check up on him. When he turned around, and I saw what my dad had done, I couldn't believe it. When I saw him, OMG, his face looked even worse than mine! I actually felt a little bad for him. Just a little bad. That was the last time I saw Blondy. We broke up and never got back together again.

Back to the haircut incident. After my father cut off my hair that day, he pulled up at my mom's job to pick her up. She jumped in the passenger seat. Bella and I were sitting in the backseat. I know my mom was already very upset about him beating me up so badly the day before, but she still had no idea what he did to me that morning when he threw that water bucket on me while I was sleeping.

When she turned around to check on me, her jaw almost fell off. She looked at my dad and started yelling at him. He totally ignored her. He knew she didn't have the power to do anything about it. She could only bark, not bite. He knew she would never leave him, which was true.

The funny thing was, he told my mom he gave me a messed up short haircut on purpose, to make me look ugly and take my beauty away from me, so no guy will look at me ever again. I can't stress enough how much of a mess it was. It was totally chopped up.

My mom, brother, sister, and all my friends felt so bad for me. My friends would contact me by calling our house phone or stop by while my dad was at work. The rest of the world had not seen me yet because he was still locking me in the house. I was locked in my father's personal prison, and he made sure that no one would see me like that, because the government could take me away from home.

Another day passed. I saw my mother walking through the door with shopping bags. She'd gone to the beauty supply store and bought some hair extensions for me. She had me sit on the floor, and she braided my hair, so I would have long hair again. She assured me I would look even prettier. She did such a great job! Just as she'd promised, I looked even better than before.

I love my mother to death. I've never met a person with so much patience and so much hope and belief. I know God will always be with her because her heart is so pure.

CHAPTER 5
I'M OUT

That same crazy summer, my favorite aunt from Tunisia, Aunt Sophia, came to visit us in Germany. She flew in right after all the craziness happened. She never really got along with my father. She never agreed with his way of raising us, or the way he treated her sister, my mom.

Weeks passed by, and I was finally ready to return back to school. The first day I went back to school, everyone wanted to ask me questions about what happened or where I had been. No one had the nerve to approach me, though. Rumors were already in the streets.

I'd forgotten we had a state exam until I arrived at school. It was extremely hot in our classroom because we had no air conditioning. Sweat was pouring down my face, and the fact I had on a long-sleeved shirt to cover my bruises only intensified the heat. I was so hot that I pulled my sleeves up without thinking. From the neck up, I was completely healed. No more black eyes and no more busted, bleeding lips. Unfortunately, I'd forgotten that my left arm was still badly bruised.

A few days before I returned to school, my father lost it again and beat me up with the huge wooden decorator spoon which was hanging on the wall. He hit the same spot over and over again on my left arm until the spoon broke. That's when he stopped.

What was his reason? I came home one minute late from the supermarket. Exactly one minute. He'd timed me. When I walked through the door, he was standing there with an alarm clock in his hands to show me I was one minute late.

So in school, when I pulled my sleeves up, my teacher saw my bruised arm. All my teachers and the principal put two and two together and quickly figured out why I missed school for so long. They realized my father had lied to them about my absences being due to a stomach virus. It was obvious that I was being physically abused at home.

We finished that class exam, and the bell was ringing for our next lunch break. I was not in the mood to eat. I'd lost my appetite a long time ago, and I was hanging out in the schoolyard.

I saw my teacher walking over to me. He asked if I

had a minute to talk to him. I said, sure. He looked into my eyes and asked if I was ok. My teacher also said he knew I would never miss school because I loved school. I was such a nerd. He also said that I was one of his best students, and even when I was sick, I still used to come to school.

"Ramla, what really happened to you? Why do you have a bruised arm? I saw the bruise on your arm," he asked me.

Oh no, I think it's time to tell the world. I think it's time to face whatever is going to happen from now on, it's time. I lied to cover for my father because I loved him. I never wanted him to get in trouble, but by now, I was exhausted from hiding, lying, crying, and sneaking. I was tired of what was going on in my house. I was tired of everything at that point.

I broke down in front of my teacher. I cried so hard that I couldn't talk. It felt like someone was choking me. It took a minute for me to get the entire story out.

My teacher made me talk to a school counselor, who was also my drama teacher. Thank God for her. This made it much easier for me to talk because I knew she would not say anything until I told her to. I felt safe with her. She took notes and wanted me to go with her to talk to a social worker outside of the school as soon as possible. She told me their job was to help me and confessed that everyone in school was talking about me. It was just a matter of time until the truth came to light, and the rumors would end.

When I returned to school, all the teachers were focused on me. They all knew my father was abusing me and finally understood why I was getting so angry in school. Everyone wanted to help me out of my situation.

When I came home after school, my Aunt Sophia opened the door for me.

"Ramla come sit down. I need to talk to you about something." I did as she said. "When you were in school earlier, I overheard your father talking to your mother."

What she heard was my father's plan. We were all going back to Tunisia for a vacation in a few days. "Your father's going to steal your passport while in Tunisia and keep you over there for good."

That meant I would be stuck in Africa and never return to Germany. Just in case you don't know, Tunisia is a third world country. It's ok for vacation, but not to spend the rest of your life. That was definitely not in my plan. As if it couldn't get worse, she told me what she heard next. He told my mother he was going to cut out my tongue with a razor so I couldn't speak again. Oh my god! That was the last straw for me. At this point, I didn't care if my mom was leaving him or not, I told myself, I AM OUT. That was the push I needed to pack my stuff and run away.

I always said to myself, *I got this, I will be ok. God is with me.* I told my aunt that I already spoke with my teachers about what happened to me. I was planning to run away that day. She said go for it, and she had my back. She suggested we tell my mom so I could say goodbye to her. My father was still at work without my mom that day, which was actually perfect. I had time to say goodbye to her in peace.

I called Brittney and told her it was time. I packed a few things. Brittney and her father were waiting to take me to a youth women's shelter. Thank God my best friends Brittney and Jenny did their best to make me happy and help me keep a positive attitude. Those girls were always there for me. Even Brittney's father got involved. They all started to research and find ways to help me get into a better living situation.

I said goodbye to my mom. I kissed her, told her I loved her, and that this was the best thing to do. I asked my mom to pack her stuff and run away with me. I told her she shouldn't be scared. Someone would help us. My mom did not have the nerve to leave with me because she was too afraid of my father. She wished me all the best and assured me we would stay in touch somehow. Mind you, back then, in 1994, there were no cell phones around, only house phones. I didn't say goodbye to my siblings because they were outside playing at the park.

That was a turning point for my life. I always thought there was no way out and that I'd just have to accept this life until I died. That was my mindset then. I felt like if I stayed, I would be dead soon. Death has a stench, and I didn't want any part of it.

Walking out the door with no fear, I actually felt relieved. There was no reason for me to turn around at all. My destination was Brittney's house, which was a block away. Brittney and her father were waiting for me outside. We jumped on the bus and drove to the shelter.

When we arrived at the shelter, the office was already closed. We needed to go to the emergency entrance. I was waiting in the lobby, and Brittney's father filled out all the paperwork for me. I felt so much happier already, not a bit of sadness.

He came back and said that the youth women's shelter was packed, and they had no more room for me. I was like, *No way! That is not right. I didn't do all this to go back home. My father is already home by now, and he got the message that I ran away. I would rather commit suicide than go back home.*

The staff member came back to us and said there was one spot left in the infant/toddler shelter. They asked if I would be ok with that. *Really? Hellooooo, of course, I will be ok with that! I would be ok sleeping with lions, snakes, rats, or crocodiles at this point! I'd be ok sharing a room with a monster. Just please don't send me back home!!* So I was with these cute infants and toddlers until the shelter director had a spot open, and they could move me to the youth women's shelter.

Hours later, they gave me a room. I remember it was a huge, bright room, but it felt so empty and small. It reminded me of a hospital trauma room.

I missed my mother and siblings. I was glad I had some company, but Brittney and her father were not allowed to stay any longer because visiting hours were over. We said our goodbyes and I went back into my room. It was cold and unwelcoming. All I wanted to do was sleep, to get this day over with.

The next day, I needed to go to school, which was around the corner from my house. I used to walk to school, but now because of where I was living, I needed to take public transportation. My school was exactly an hour away from me now, but fears flooded my mind. *What am I supposed to do if I run into my father? Is he going to shoot me? Is he carrying his gun with him?* All these questions were running through my mind while I was sitting on the bus on my way to school to take my exams.

It didn't matter what I was going through, school was always the number one priority for me. I never used excuses to cut school, even with all the issues I had at home. It made me study even harder to show my father I would be somebody special one day.

I heard he told my mother if I ever ran away, I would end up as a junky, a prostitute, or homeless. I remember thinking, *Wow. This is how much hope you have when it comes to your daughter?* At that point, I decided I wanted to be the most successful person on earth. I've kept what he said in the back of my mind. When I think about it now, I am who I am because of what he did to me. It has made me who I am today.

My other goal was to prove that my father was wrong about how he raised us. I refused to continue his cycle. If I ever had kids, I would never ever put my hands on them. I couldn't imagine beating up a kid, EVER.

Living in the shelter was crazy. All of the kids were without a mother or father. It was very sad. I felt so bad for these little kids. *Who's going to hug them when they get sick? Who's going to kiss them or love them in general?* I tried to spend most of my time with them, just giving them my love.

I remember there were five siblings on my floor, and they all were of different nationalities. They were Chinese, German, Russian, Indian, and African. They all were one year apart, which meant each year their mother was dating a man of a different nationality, having a baby, and dropping it off at the shelter. Life can be so unfair. At least those siblings had each other, and hopefully, they would find a family to adopt all of them so they will not be separated.

A week after I stayed in the toddler shelter, one of the workers came up to me and called me to the office. They said that they'd spoken to my father and he wanted me back home. She informed me that the law in Germany states if a child is a first-time runaway, they have to send the child back home. Once back home, maybe the family can make it work. If a child runs away a second time and returns to the shelter, they will not be sent home again. Since it was my FIRST time running away, the law said they had to send me back to hell.

WHAT?! No one told me that. How was I supposed to know that? Oh my God. Does it mean everything I did and planned to run away from home was for nothing? Does it mean I'm still not free yet? I have to go back to my abusive father? What if he kills me this time? I can't believe this. Now he can fulfill his plan to leave me there when we go on vacation? Plus, cut my tongue off? GOD help me.

They sent me home. They made sure that the social worker was in the house too. When I arrived, I saw my father and the social worker in the living room on the couch, waiting to have a conversation with me. It was a lot of blah, blah, blah, and then the social worker left.

So I was back there. My mom and siblings were happy to have me back, but my father ignored me. He actually did not hit me again, but he was doing other things to mess with me mentally.

CHAPTER 6
DON'T TAKE ME

Life went on. I was 16 years old now. I had a part-time job at a hair salon in Wandsbek, Germany as an assistant, or shampoo girl. The name of the place was Struwwelpeter. I loved it there! Everyone was so kind to me, and the pay was very good. I was the best at what I was doing, which was shampooing the clients' hair, preparing them for color, and taking care of the towels, by washing, drying and folding them. I made sure I always did the towels when the salon wasn't busy.

The salon owner had his laundry room in the basement of the salon. One day, I walked downstairs by myself to get the clean towels, and there was a woman dressed in all white. She wore a white jacket and white pants. She was standing next to the washing machine doing nothing. She just stood there looking at me.

Her hair was in a mullet haircut, short on top and long in the back. When I saw her, I screamed and jumped. My heart started racing. I knew right away, this wasn't right.

I ran back upstairs and told everyone in the salon that a woman dressed in white was downstairs in the basement, right next to the washing machine. I stood there, shaking. They all looked at me like, *What???*

One of the hairstylists went downstairs to check, and when she came back upstairs, she said no one was down there. Then the owner went to check, and he also said no one was down there. *Ok. Maybe I'm just hallucinating.* I told them I wouldn't go back down there until I recovered from what I knew I saw.

I shampooed the last client's hair and clocked out. I walked to the bus stop. It was a freezing cold winter and was already dark by 6 p.m. when I left. I sat on the bench, waiting for my bus, still thinking about what had just happened. *That lady looked so real. But what was she? A ghost? A soul or what? Was it something good or something evil?* I was so scared and confused. I decided right away to pray.

Right in front of me was the street and a bush. I started staring at the bush. Seconds later, I saw her again. She was sitting *in* the bush! She had the same white jacket, white pants, and the same mullet hairstyle. I even remember her hair color. It was like an orange auburn, and she was probably in her mid-fifties.

When I saw her, I closed my eyes and continued to pray. When my friend's mom walked to the station and said hey, I was so happy! I was glad to see someone at the bus stop with me that I actually knew. I didn't tell her what I'd seen, because at that point, I didn't know how anyone would react. I was not crazy. I saw her sitting in the bush-right there. The bus finally came. I sat with my friend's mom all the way in the back of the bus. I looked out of the window to check the bush again, and the woman was gone. I was in shock. I can't even tell you if I even had a conversation with my friend's mom. I was out of it.

The bus ride took almost 30 minutes. I reached my stop, got out, and started to walk home. It was dark. I kept turning back to see if the woman in white was following me. A few minutes later, I turned around, and she was standing there! She was far away, but she was there. It was almost like a scene from the horror movie, *The Ring*. I started to run. I was running so fast, I could not breathe. I rang all the apartment bells until I was let into my building. I didn't even wait for the elevator. I ran up the stairs to our place on the third floor. My mom opened the door.

"Why are you breathing like that? Are you ok?"

At that moment, I thought, *Thank God my dad took me to have my asthma healed, otherwise I probably would have died today.* I told my mom about the woman dressed in white. My mom wasn't surprised.

"Did she touched you?" my mom asked.

"No," I replied.

"Did you touch her?"

"No."

"Ok. Listen to me, Ramla. If you ever see her again, don't go to her. If she calls you over to her, don't go. Don't let her touch you. Ever."

I thought, *Why? And what is happening here?* She told me that the woman was dead, and she was either a gin or a ghost, and if she called me and I went to her and touched her, I WOULD DIE. *Ok. So now at least I know what is going on. Only God can help here.*

I prayed myself to sleep that night. That was the first and last time something like that happened to me. I never saw the women in white again.

Now, if you are wondering if I was high or drunk or

swallowed any pills, the answer is NO. I know people start to hallucinate if they're on drugs, but let me tell you something. I was sober and normal as a human being can be. Again, I believe in healers sent by God. If someone told me they heard or saw things the rest of us didn't see, I'd believe them, because we are not the only ones on this planet. Also, I know for a fact that animals and babies can see those things too! With that being said, I'll leave it at that.

CHAPTER 7
DEATH BEFORE DISHONOR

One morning I woke up to get myself ready for school. It was just my father and me at home. My mother had gone to work already, and my brother was already in school. I can't even remember where my sister was, maybe still sleeping.

I usually make my own breakfast, but that day, my dad was already sitting by the table reading his newspaper. I walked by him to wash up and then walked to the kitchen to make my breakfast. Then I heard his voice. I couldn't really see his face, because it was behind the newspaper. The funny thing was I knew he was illiterate, so I realized he was looking at the pictures, pretending to read.

"Sit down. There's no need to make your breakfast. I made it for you already, just how you like it. Toast with jelly and cheese. Coffee with milk and sugar on the side".

*Ok…*That was super weird to me because he never *ever* made my breakfast. Something was fishy. I looked at that sandwich that he made me, and it was molded all over. The entire slice of bread was green. I was like, *Is he serious?*

Now I'm taking the bread, cutting it into pieces and hiding it in my bra, pretending to chew and swallow it. I picked up my coffee cup to take a sip and saw lots of weird bluish bubbles on the surface. I tried to take my spoon and stir the bubbles, but they just kept popping back up to the surface. Right then and there, I knew 100% that my father was trying to poison me.

I ran into the kitchen with the cup, leaving him sitting behind that newspaper. The kitchen was just one step behind me. I poured everything in the sink. He actually was still sitting there and did not say a word. I went into my room, got dressed, and went to school.

I could not stop thinking about what had just happened. *He was trying to kill me! Just like that. For what? What did I actually do to him for him to hate me like that?* He was my father, which made everything even more confusing to me.

After school, I went home and found my mother at home alone, cleaning the kitchen. At that exact moment, I remembered we'd had lots of little bugs by the windows, and no one was able to get rid of them. I walked inside the kitchen to talk to my mother and I saw blue powder all over the window. I noticed all those bugs were lying there dead.

I asked my mom what kind of powder it was. She explained that my dad just sprinkled it on the windows to get rid of the bugs and they were dead in just seconds.

I put two and two together and rushed to make coffee. I sprinkled the blue powder from the window into my coffee cup, and sure enough, it was the same weird bluish bubbles popping up to the surface that I'd seen that morning in the cup he'd made me.

I actually planned not to tell my mother about it, but I changed my mind.

"Take a look at this. Do you see this on top of my coffee?"

"Yes."

I told her everything about how dad was trying to kill me with this.

"Where is he hiding this blue powder?"

"Inside the safe in the big closet. No one has the keys or combination to the safe but your father."

My mother knew my father was a psycho and totally believed me. She stopped what she was doing and sat down. She was just sitting there with a blank look on her face. She could not believe he was actually trying to poison me.

"Ramla, do you know if you would have drunk that coffee you would be dead by now?"

"Yes." Now we had another reason to plan my next runaway. This time we knew by law, they could not send me back home again because it would be the second time I ran away.

CHAPTER 8
MISFITS

I went back to that shelter the next morning by myself. At this point, it was normal for me. My heartbeat wasn't racing anymore, and it was like I was going to visit a friend. I was back in the same shelter, and this time they had a spot available for me in the women's youth department with teenagers closer to my age. This time they actually kept me there. No one was going to tell me there was a law that would send me back home. With that being said, I didn't see my dad for the next EIGHT YEARS. That's another story on its own.

It was wild in there. I saw a lot. One time I was talking to a 12-year-old, and he was smoking weed during the entire conversation. I told him that he was way too young for that. His answer was that he was born with weed in his mouth instead of a pacifier.

I met a young girl in the shelter who was a

prostitute. She was spending all her money on drugs. Out of all the kids in that place, I can honestly say I was the only one sitting in that mess studying for my upcoming exams.

Those who were running the shelter noticed that I was different and knew I needed to get out of there as soon as possible before I fell into a dark hole like all the other kids in there. Usually, you need to be in the shelter for years until they consider you ready to live on your own or ready to be in a group home.

A group home or youth housing is called "Jugendwohnung" in German. It was pretty much an apartment or a house from the government that needs to be shared by two or three other teenagers. We call them roommates.

Living in a group home for a homeless or an abused teenager was a big deal in Germany, especially when you came from a shelter. It was levels up and way more luxurious. A better lifestyle all around and almost like a real HOME.

Some of the group homes had one or two social workers. Social workers either lived there with you, watching the teenagers or worked there Monday through Friday, from 9 am to 5 pm.

In my group home, they were available until 5 pm and were gone on the weekends. With no adults around, we were free to be teenagers. After one month of being in the shelter, I got called to the office and asked if I was ready to leave.

"Ramla, your time has come to leave. We hope you will like the place we've chosen for you. You deserve this one." They wanted to know if I could see myself living in a group home and being on my own. They had a spot open in a beautiful house in Steilshoop (a district in Hamburg, Germany), and if I was interested, to take a look at it.

I think they really liked me because all those shelter kids could not believe that I was ready to move out. I'd just moved in! On the other hand, none of these shelter kids hated on me. They actually all loved me. They helped me pack and also helped me move my stuff. They understood that I needed my peace, and I was a good kid looking to do the right thing. And would you believe it? After all that drama in my life, I still graduated high school with an A+!

CHAPTER 9
GROUP HOME

The van was packed with my belongings, and I was looking out the window while they were driving me to my new home. I was about to move in, then a wave of fear washed over my mind. *What if the girls, also called my new roommates, will not like me? What if I will not like them?*

We parked the van in front of the huge house. It was a beautiful, newly constructed building and was probably the nicest house I've ever seen. Downstairs was a daycare, and the entire upstairs was for us. I loved it! It was stunning, breathtaking, and so luxurious.

They showed me my room. It was a good size, but not the biggest room. *Of course not. I should not complain. I'm the newest girl in here, so I should wait my turn until I can move to a bigger room.*

The social worker introduced me to the girls. They

were all nice. I remember Tina. She was a kickboxer and was very dedicated to her sport. She was kind and very professional. Then there was Sara, a blonde girl with no personality. She only cared about her boyfriend, but at least she was nice and friendly. There was a third girl. She was about to move out soon because she was turning 18. I can't really remember her name because I might have lived with her for a couple of days. Overall, she was never really there, so I forgot about her.

When you turn 18, you leave the group home and move into your own apartment. But usually, the social workers did all that work for you and helped you out. They made sure all your needs were taken care of, from money to work to living arrangements.

I loved my new home, and the girls became my family. I joined kickboxing with Tina three times a week. I signed up for a trade school, which would go for two years. But first, I needed to enjoy my summer break.

I loved my new life. I also found a summer job in an ice cream joint in the city. That job was paying a lot of money per day. I was 16 years old with lots of cash in my pockets, and I did not know what to do with it. I always had a good-paying job, as far as I remember. When it came to that, I was blessed and thankful. That's how I became spoiled in life later on, and I refused to work a low-paying job, ever. Sorry, not sorry.

I started kickboxing three times a week. Tina got me hooked on it, and besides that, I had my school. I was actually a very good girl. Just school, study, and practice. Kickboxing taught me how to be disciplined, respectful, and taught me how to defend myself.

I used to see red flags back in the days when I used to live with my father. If someone pushed me or talked shit about me, or gave me a look that I didn't like, I was on them. I didn't even give bullies time to explain themselves. I ran after them and beat them down just like that. If I was in a good mood, I might let them explain themselves afterward.

Sooner or later, everyone knew the name RAMLA. They used to say, don't mess with that one! She is crazy! I wanted to help anyone who was bullied. I would beat a bully down with no excuse. That's how I gained my respect in the streets.

At that point, I was on my own, and I was respected on the street. Every guy wanted to date me. Some guys were too shy to try to talk to me. They knew how selective I'd become. I was very picky and didn't want it to settle for a loser. I didn't need any more headaches in my life. I started to love and enjoy my life. But that didn't last for long.

CHAPTER 10
STEVE

Other than Brittney and Jenny, I had another best friend, whose name was Steve. Yes, he was a boy, and if I wasn't around Brittney or Jenny, I was around him and did boyish things.

Steve always brought the tomboy attitude out of me. He became my best friend. I met him just a few weeks before I ran away from home. We used to do a lot of crazy things together. Steve was a badass and a street kid. He almost had the same past as me. He ran away from home way before I did. The streets made us a family, and that's how we became best friends. He watched my back and made sure that I was taken care of like a little sister. I did the same for him.

Even though I ran away from my neighborhood, which was like an hour away, I never lost contact with Steve. I pretty much lost contact with Brittney and Jenny. It was almost like out of sight out of mind, but not with Steve. He always made sure that I was ok and around. I was one of his crew members. He made sure to know who I was hanging out with and if I had enough food on the table. He always looked after me whenever I had a problem with someone. Steve was a drug dealer and a hustler.

He lived only for today, never tomorrow, which is the total opposite of me. I was always thinking about and planning for the future. He got locked up several times. I was never arrested or committed any crime. I became his balance. To this day, he calls me his guardian angel.

Because Steve was someone who only lived for the moment, he did a lot of things without thinking. I helped him out of a few situations he had in the past. I wanted to be there for him. I felt like God gave me that purpose. In my heart, I saw him like a brother or my child. I needed to look after him.

Steve was dating at least three girls at the same time, all the time. One was never enough for him. It was like he had a disease. One girlfriend, let's call her #1, used to show up in the morning, then she left. Girlfriend #2 showed up in the afternoon, then left. In the evening, girlfriend #3 was ready to stop by.

Some of them knew about each other. Some of them

thought they were the only one. I felt bad for all those girls, but he was my best friend and I had his back. He knew that I would never snitch on him.

I remember one day we all went out clubbing at SKYY. I saw one of Steve's girlfriends outside crying. Her name was Vicky. I asked her why she is so upset, and she told me that he'd hit her and taken her house keys from her. She begged me to talk to him and to get her keys back.

She said I was the only one he listened to. It was true; whatever decisions he used to make, he asked me first. If I said yes, he did it. If I said no, he let it go. It was kind of cute that a crazy street respected gangster-like him would listen to little ol' me. I was the only one that could tame him. Maybe he saw the mother in me that he had always been looking for.

I was actually mad at Steve. How could he put his hands on a woman? Especially after he knew all my history about Blondy and my father.

I wasn't thinking anymore. I saw a red flag. I walked back inside the club to look for Steve, and when I saw him, I smacked him in the face. I took Vicky's keys and pocketbook and walked away. He was in shock. He did not expect me to do this, but he respected me.

While walking away, Steve yelled, "Tell her I'm

done with her." I returned her things to her, told her to find a better guy for herself, and that my best friend wasn't good for her.

I did not speak to Steve for a minute. I started dating my friend's cousin, Thomas. He was so boring, but I thought, *Let me give it a try*. Steve found out we were dating, and when he saw Thomas at a nightclub one day, he destroyed his face. I was like *WTF??? Since when are we on that kind of jealousy level? That never happened before.*

I realized I was never dating anyone during my friendship with him. As soon as I broke up with Blondy, I met Steve. After Blondy, I needed a long break from boys. I was just scared of relationships.

I was home in the kitchen cooking, and my bell rang. My roommate Tina answered the door. When I turned around, I saw Steve and his cousin Ed standing in my kitchen with lots of grocery bags in their hands.

He'd gone food shopping for me, which was very kind of him. He always cared about me when it came to stuff like that. He always made sure that my fridge was full.

I asked about that Thomas incident at the nightclub, but he ignored me. Thomas was not my type anyway, and he couldn't fight. Loser. If a man can't protect himself, how can he protect me? So I pretty much dumped Thomas.

Steve ignored me when I asked him that question again, so I let it go. That dude wasn't worth talking about anyway. Now his cousin Ed was in my kitchen trying to flirt with me? I saw Steve's face changing; he did not like it.

All this time, I thought he was getting jealous because he wanted to protect me as a sister, but I was getting the feeling he liked me, maybe a little too much. What is it? He made sure to get rid of his cousin as soon as possible.

After his cousin left, he looked at me and started to open up to me. He said he always saw me like his sister that he never had. But now I was changing and becoming a young woman, and he didn't see me like a sister anymore. I was becoming his type of woman. He admitted he was very jealous when he found out about Thomas and me, and that's why he needed to stop it. He knew Thomas was scared of him and that Thomas would never talk to me again after that. Steve also admitted that it broke his heart when he saw his cousin trying to flirt with me.

Steve confessed he had a crush on me. He asked if I wanted to be his girl. He said, "Let's try it out, you will not regret it." He said that he would never treat me like all those other girls. He never felt love for them, but with me, it so much different. He said he actually felt pure love.

Now what? I was speechless. *I do not feel the same for him. I'm not in love with him, not even a tiny bit. I still see him as my very best friend and brother. Do I look stupid, starting a relationship with Steve? Everyone knows he is my BFF, and on top of that, he is a player–an abusive player.*

He was sitting in front of me, staring at me with puppy dog eyes, waiting for an answer. Guess what? I said ok, because at the end of the day, who got me more than him? He was already my family. We had each other's back, and if he tried to play me, I would kill him, simple as that. I took the chance because I loved to take challenges like that. *Plus, he can't be worse than Blondy or my father, right???*

It took me almost six months to fall in love with Steve. He knew that. He was on cloud nine with me. It was never a dull moment with him, always fun and active. When I first met his mother, I fell in love with her. She was a beautiful soul. I also fell in love with Steve's culture, which was from Ghana. The food, especially their dish fufu, got me hooked. He cooked almost every day for me.

He drove me to school and picked me up from school. He really did everything for me, and I could tell it came from his heart. If someone showed me how to be spoiled, it was him.

I made sure I helped him out as much as I could when it came to him becoming a good man and a good person overall. I also tried very hard to get him off the streets and stop selling drugs.

I signed him up at a driving school to get his driver's license because he was always driving without one. I made sure he went to all his driving sessions. Eventually, he earned his driver's license, and he was so happy. He told me that it was the first time in his life where he felt like he accomplished something.

A few months went by, and we got engaged. We were so happy. Everyone was jealous of us. We were "that" couple. They used to call us Bonnie and Clyde.

Time passed, and I noticed a huge change in Steve. He got irritated fast. He'd never shown that side to me. I felt like I didn't need to babysit anyone. If I wanted to do good with my life, I had to think about me.

As more time passed by, I felt he was not the one for me. I was a nerd, a good kid, actually an angel. He was still a street kid, a drug dealer, the devil. Our nickname changed in a heartbeat on the streets.

It went from Bonnie and Clyde to angel vs. devil. I thought, *If I give him an ultimatum to have a normal life and stop selling drugs, or I will leave him. I can't have a man like him being a good role model for my future children.* The street was talking, and I heard that he got hooked on cocaine. Now it made sense why he went from zero to 100 so quick.

CHAPTER 11
BFF

I started to release myself from this toxic relationship with Steve. I was trying to leave him step by step and started to do my own thing. In the beginning, Steve and I were glued together. I began to go out more without him and make new friends.

I met this girl Alina who was also street famous. We were mentally so connected that everyone started to say that she was the cheese to my cheeseburger. I got off the bus one day and saw Alina on the other side of the street. She called me over and asked me if I want to go with her, her sister Mimi, and some friends to Amsterdam.

I am a Sagittarius, and everyone knows we are super spontaneous, so I said, "Ok, let's go." That's how our friendship started. She became my best friend to this day. I was so happy to find my soulmate, Alina. She was just as crazy as me, spontaneous like me, and so much fun. I had no problems when I was with her. Even now, she is my rock and my number one supporter.

Amsterdam was awesome. It was my first time there, and I loved it. I remember we went on a ferry, and it was a beautiful hot summer day. We enjoyed the breeze, and we had so much fun that we didn't want to get off. We drove back and forth all day until the sun went down. We were so super high. I finally had a moment where I felt like nothing was bothering me. I didn't have to be scared to rush home or have to explain myself to anybody. I felt FREE. I *was* FREE for once. I felt comfortable and secure with Alina and her friends.

After we got off the ferry, we visited a festival then went back to Germany. We made sure to leave on time because we didn't want to miss partying at our favorite nightclub, SKYY. That club was popping every Friday night! If you couldn't get into club SKYY, then you were a nobody back in the day. Amsterdam is only three hours away from Hamburg, Germany. So it became a habit for us to go to Amsterdam for a few days whenever we got bored then come back to Germany.

Steve did not hear from me the entire time I was in Amsterdam. That Friday night, we left Germany to go to Amsterdam. He knew we would show up at club SKYY. Steve never liked Alina. He knew from our outings that I would listen more to her than I would listen to him. Also, she always saw right through his bullshit.

Alina told me she never understood why I ever got involved with him and that I should know better because he was no good. As his best friend, I should have definitely known better. But I told her that he'd changed and she should be around us to witness it herself.

After I'd left home. I lost contact with Brittney and Jenny. I was really lonely, with no family or friends except for Steve and Alina. I wanted them to get along. I felt like they were all I had left. They were the only people I considered family. She was my best friend, and he was my man, so them getting along wasn't too much to ask, right?

CHAPTER 12
KIDNAPPED

Alina was worrying too much about me. She knew that Steve was on cocaine and that he lost his temper quickly. She never wanted him to put his hands on me–ever.

Every year, there was a big concert going on at the "Markthalle" in Hamburg City. By the time the concert came around, I wasn't talking to Steve anymore. I'd finally found the courage to end the relationship with him.

After I left the concert, I was walking by myself, to catch the next taxi a block away. While I was walking, I noticed a car following me. The car was driving very slowly, maybe 5 mph. It was around walking speed. I stopped to see who was in the car. It was Steve! He told me to jump in the car, and he would drive me home. I refused to get in his car. I ignored him and kept walking to the taxi stand. I turned around and begged him very politely to please leave me alone.

That did not work out very well.

He got out of the car, grabbed me, pulled me into the car, and sped off. The person that I saw that day was not Steve. He was possessed, completely controlled by an evil spirit. It was the devil himself. Even his voice changed like in those horror movies.

I told myself just to be quiet and be nice to him because who knew what was on his crazy mind. He drove me to his friend's house in the neighborhood "Horn". It was a very rough neighborhood. His friend lived on the top floor of a six-story building with no elevator.

Inside the apartment, there was junk everywhere. Everyone in the apartment was high from doing cocaine that was on the table. This was more than a trap house, it was a drug house.

I was no angel. I'd smoked cigarettes from time to time. I'd even tried marijuana, but that was it. I would never play with the devil's toys or the devil's ingredients, especially when it comes to cocaine or anything in that category. I mean, look what it did to Steve! He was almost on the right track, but whoever he was associating himself with dragged him into a dark hole.

The apartment Steve took me to belonged to his friend, Troy. Troy was one of those many guys trying to date and talk to me. After I realized he took me to Troy's crib, I thought, *Oh my God, this is going to be a super funny situation. How do you call yourself his friend, but behind his back, you're trying to talk to his girl?* Steve would've killed him if I told him that, but I stayed quiet to save Troy's life.

Steve was ready to leave the building and told Troy to watch me and not let me leave the apartment.

He yelled at everyone inside the apartment, "If she escapes, I'm killing everyone in here, that I promise!"

I got kidnapped, now I'm being held hostage. Why me? Haven't I been through enough shit in my life? Now this! This was 100% kidnapping plain and simple.

Did I fail to mention that Steve, for the first time in our relationship, put his hands on me? He beat me down in front of everyone in the living room. There were at least ten people in that place, and not one came to help! They just watched Steve beat on me. They were scared of Steve. *Hello???? A girl is getting beat down, right in front of your face!* I realized I was on my own.

Steve did all that because I wanted to break up with him. Blondy popped into my mind during the entire beating. I had already been through this with Blondy and my father. *Is this the circle that I will always be in? Am I a magnet to problems?* I cried and screamed.

All of them were losers in my eyes. All these losers were taking orders from someone who beats up on women. *You ain't no man, you're just scared little boys.* They weren't men, they were pussies! There wasn't one *man* in the apartment. He used to call them his runners, corner boys. Whatever you want to call them, they were his slaves.

After Steve left the apartment, I started planning my escape. As I was crying in the kitchen, Troy came over to calm me down.

I asked Troy, "How can you say that you got a crush on me, and let Steve beat on me? You witnessed with your own eyes. Are you ok with that? Why didn't you help me? How are you a real man, watching another man beating up a woman? How could I ever consider you being my man? You have proven yourself to be a zero." Now he was acting like, oh, I wanted to help you, but blah, blah, blah. I didn't want to hear any of that shit.

My plan was to trick Troy into getting me something to eat because I was starving. Since Troy was feeling so miserable for not helping me, he left the apartment to go get me some food. It was supposed to be his way of making it up to me.

While Troy was gone, I was left with a bunch of crack heads. They were so high they didn't notice I was still in the apartment. I ran to the balcony for help and saw a child playing outside. I grabbed some change from the table and threw it down to get the kid's attention. I couldn't scream, because I didn't want to wake the zombies. So after getting the kid's attention, I told him to get his father and tell him to call the police because I've been kidnapped.

The kid was on point. He did exactly what I told him. Two minutes later, an entire SWAT team stormed the apartment. Unfortunately for Steve, he was arriving back at the wrong time. They arrested him for kidnapping.

I can't remember how long Steve was in jail, but it definitely wasn't long enough. I felt horrified when I heard he was out. I still could not believe he'd put his hands on me. After all I'd been through and after everything he knew about my past? After the kidnapping, I requested an order of protection, so Steve could not be within 100 yards of me. He was not allowed to come near me at all.

One girl in the group home was moving out, which

meant I could finally move into the biggest room in the house. We had a new girl moving in. Her name was Sandy.

Sandy was funny in the beginning, and we all liked her. After a couple of months, I found out that she was a fake bitch and a real good snitch.

After breaking up with Steve, I began dating a nice guy named George. George was a good balance for me. He took me mentally away from Steve, which was what I needed at the time. I wasn't interested in George, I just needed a distraction from Steve, or to make him jealous of George. Whatever it was, I was only using him. Yes, I said it. For the first time, I felt malicious, like I wanted to get all my anger out on someone or something. Poor George was in the line of fire.

There was nothing sexual going on. George was in love with me, but I knew how to handle him without him getting out of control and getting to that level. Everyone at the group home knew about George. They were actually happy because no one liked Steve after he hit me. So you can say I finally moved on.

After graduating from high school, I went to trade school. Trade school was hard. I found myself studying every day just to keep up. I started doing hair extensions on the side at home. After school, I was doing the girls' hair from school at the group home.

I found a good side job after school. It was in the city at an Italian cafe selling ice cream. While at work sitting at the counter looking out the window, I saw Steve walk toward me and look me straight in the eyes. I screamed for Steve to leave my job and that I would never give him another chance. Steve dragged me out of the ice cream section which was in a café, and the café was in a mall. He threw me into his car, AGAIN. He drove me to another friend's house.

As soon as we entered the upstairs apartment, I saw Steve taken off his belt, and I knew what was about to happen. He proceeded to beat me with his belt. I was so confused because he had kidnapped me again, and now he's beating me with a belt? What is happening here?

We broke up. I have the right to move on and date whoever I want. While I was crying on the floor, I felt no pain at all. I was numb to all of Steve's abuse because of what I went through with my father. Steve picked me up and apologized for beating me again. He couldn't believe I'd moved on so fast.

I asked him what he was talking about. He said a little birdie told him I was seeing George. I really wanted to know who this birdie was. I begged him to tell me. *Who was this spy giving Steve this information? Once I find out who the snitch is, their funeral will be arranged.* I got back with Steve after he apologized. There were two reasons I got back with Steve. One, to find this rat who was telling all my business. Second, to exact my revenge against Steve.

What is wrong with me? Is my mind that fucked up? I thought he loved me, why does he keep beating on me? I made excuses for him. I told myself, *These men can't talk, so they hit.*

Steve told me he went to my crib to look for me and met my new sneaky roommate, Sandy. I was in shock. Not because she snitched, but that she didn't care about what would happen to her if I found out? Who knows, maybe she had a crush on him. Steve actually offered her ten euros for information on me. *Really? Are you that broke? Are you that hungry?* Ten euros and she told him everything. At the end of the day, it didn't matter. I wasn't with Steve, so why saying anything? My blood was boiling because Sandy had put herself all in my business.

Don't you know who I am? That's ok. You should have done your research before you started messing with me, baby. I'm on my way to you now.

When you move into a group home, you become sisters, a family member, automatically. Family doesn't snitch on each other–period. Sandy wasn't family. Real family knew there was a possibility Steve could lose his temper. Because of her, I was embarrassed, dragged, kidnapped, and beaten with a belt.

I told Steve that I was good and understood why he reacted that way. Now back together, I asked him to please drive me home. On the drive home, my mind was racing about what to do with Sandy. I did not tell Steve what I had in mind for her.

The ride home took much longer than usual. It takes about 20 minutes, but it felt like hours. At this point, I was shaking and couldn't wait to put hands on Sandy. All the drama I went through earlier? Sandy was about to feel two times worse.

When Steve parked the car, I told him I needed to use the bathroom and ran upstairs. I went to her door and busted it open. Luckily for her, she wasn't there.

I walked to Tina's room, where Sandy was sitting on the couch, drinking a gallon of milk. Walking right up to her, I asked her if I can have it. She handed me the carton, then I proceeded to pour it all over her head. Then I started to fuck her up.

I can't explain to you what happened. I was in such a rage. It took Tina, who is built like a man, and Steve to drag me off of her before I killed her. After several minutes, they finally were able to pull me off. I can say I felt so much better after beating her ass. God, I sounded like my father after he beat up Blondy.

I didn't get into any trouble from my social workers because it was 100% Sandy's fault. Everyone knew Steve was violent towards me, and I was trying to escape him. The last thing I needed was Steve in my personal life, aggravating me.

Hopefully, Sandy learned something that day. I can't remember if I ever made up with her. When I cut someone out of my life, they're pretty much gone forever. It's a good and bad thing, but I'm good with that decision either way in Sandy's case.

Steve worked on himself to try to be normal again. I guess he quit that strong "baking soda". We were back to being happy. Everything was ok until one day he snapped again.

Steve had moved into his new group home, and I went to spend the night. Because of the latest event, he wasn't allowed to come over to my crib. When I woke up in the morning to leave the house, he'd locked me in the basement! At this point, I told myself I'm done with these kidnapping games.

I cried and screamed. In my frustration, I decided to destroy the basement. I was looking around for anything I could use. There was a finished kitchen in the basement. On the stove was a huge pot filled with spaghetti sauce. Then the idea hit me. In my anger, I took that entire pot and painted the walls with tomato sauce. There was nothing in the world that could've stopped me. I'd had ENOUGH.

I never stopped screaming for help. Maybe an hour passed before a dog sitter walked by and helped me climb out of the tiny window. All I can say was, *Boom! In your face, Steve! I escaped again!! You can't do anything to me.* I jumped on the bus and went to the next train station.

When I got to the train station, Steve was standing there with the strangest look on his face. His eyes were as big as baseballs. I walked right up to Steve, put my finger in his face, and I told him if he ever put hands on me again, I'd kill him. He got the message because when he saw the anger in my eyes, he knew he'd better leave me alone.

Why do guys stick on my ass like that? It's not cute or sexy. It's so annoying like mosquitos down south.

CHAPTER 13
AFRICAN LEGACY

Alina got me into an African dance group. She used to go there for years and begged me to come and join. The only thing I was doing at that time was studying and working at the ice cream shop, so why not? I needed to get my mind off Steve, so I joined. It was perfect for me because it relaxed my mind and body. I loved it, and I finally felt happy.

I'm so lucky I was born in Tunisia! Only people from Africa were allowed to be in the group. There was no exception, which made sense because the name of the group was African Legacy. I was so proud to be a part of it.

The lady who was running the class was a famous opera singer from South Africa, named Monique. Monique became like my second mother. She was such a blessing and was the one who gave me a purpose in life.

The group had three main benefits for the kids who participated. First, it got kids off the streets and gave us something to do and have a passion for. Second, it was free. Some kids couldn't afford to take part in the dance program because they were street kids. Third, we all became one big family. It was just what I needed after leaving home so early.

The group had approximately 30 dancers, ten drummers, R&B and gospel singers, actors, designers, etc. Everyone in the group had their purpose and talent. We blended together very well.

We practiced almost every day after school, and soon we were performing in huge arenas. Everyone wanted to book African Legacy for their events. We sold out shows all over Germany. We even had parts in TV shows. I started seeing money from my performances. I could not believe I was able to make so much money with one performance. Monique was overjoyed with the success of the group.

One day, Monique called a meeting to tell us about her vision to start a musical. We were excited because we loved to perform anything with singing and dancing.

She had a script prepared, and she'd written a beautiful solo for me in the play.

I played the wind, and my solo dance was breathtaking. It did not take long until we were all over the place with our musical promotion. The musical was always sold out.

I was enjoying one of the best times of my life. No drama, sadness, or worries. For once, I was protected by 30 dancers, which I called my sisters. Ten drummers, which I called my brothers, and Monique and her husband, who I called my parents.

When I was on stage, I had no problems. I felt like a newborn baby. When I embraced playing the wind, it transported me to another world. It was just me, the stage, and the drums.

Monique heard about my stressful personal relationship with Steve. She knew and liked Steve, but did not tolerate him putting his hands on me. Monique invited him to her house one afternoon to have a serious talk about me. She wanted me to be there too.

I thought, *Why not? Whatever it takes at this point to calm Steve down.* I walked in and saw Monique with her husband sitting on the couch, waiting for us. Steve walked in a few minutes later. It felt like my parents were preaching and warning Steve.

Their conversation was getting to him. He felt horrible and started to cry. He was very apologetic and promised that it would never happen again.

Oh yeah. I've heard that before…

The musical was on, and we were sold out for three months. We were performing almost every day, and Steve was by my side the entire time to support me. He was his old self again.

Monique made sure that my part had a live singer to go with my wind performance. It was her sister, who flew in from Amsterdam to sing the most beautiful African song. Those were beautiful memories.

Sadly, Monique is no longer with us, but she will forever and always hold a cherished place in our hearts.

CHAPTER 14
MY GIFT

A month before our show ended, I missed my period for almost two weeks. I had cramps, so I thought my period was coming, but it never came. I was pretty sure what was happening but didn't want to believe it. I ignored the signals in my body.

I was back with Steve, love me, or hate me. It's embarrassing at this point, even to admit that I went back to him. I always make decisions with my heart instead of using my brain. At that time, it felt right to be back with him. I was obsessed with this crazy boy.

It was upsetting to many people in my life. They'd tried their best to help me out by talking to Steve about putting his hands on me. Then as soon as they turned around, I was back with him.

Everyone gave up on me. They used to say, "I think Ramla likes that stuff", and "She loves when a man hits her. That's what she is used to."

I felt like someone was covering my mouth so I couldn't talk or scream. *How do I "love" when someone puts his hands on me? Do they know what I am actually going through deep inside? How could you say something like that? People just assume. They've never been in my shoes and will never know or experience what I've been through.*

A couple of weeks went by, and I actually was able to stay away from Steve. He was getting violent again. He went to Africa for some business, and I was actually FREE again. This time it was for a good minute. I had no contact with him. I guess he got over me too.

I was at Alina's mom's house when Alina and Mimi dragged me to the bathroom to take a home pregnancy test. Alina already had a baby girl a year prior to me. She was a young mother, and I loved her baby. *But was I ready to be a mother? A good mother? What about my dance career? What about my education? What about everything else? What about the father of my child?* I knew Steve could never be a good father (or anything close to a good father). I didn't know if I was ready for this important step.

In my mind, I had three options: raise the baby myself, have an abortion, or give the baby up for adoption.

The last two options didn't work for me. I knew in my gut it would have to be the first option. I would raise the baby on my own.

After taking the test, all I could do was wait for the results. My nerves were all over the place. There were so many questions crossing my mind. I was so scared. The time came to know the result that would change my life.

I WAS PREGNANT.

One of Steve's best friends, Marcus, knew I was taking a pregnancy test and waited for the results so he could inform Steve. Steve didn't have my new number, and I was not ready to give it to him, so we communicated through Marcus. When Marcus called to find out the results of the test, I told him that I was pregnant, but I had not decided what to do with the baby.

Everyone had an opinion. Alina was in my ear telling me to keep the baby, so our kids could grow up together. She told me that she could help me with whatever I needed. Her sister Mimi was in the other ear, telling me not to keep the baby. She said I shouldn't make the same mistake Alina did, and this could ruin the rest of my life.

I was 50/50 on my decision and had no clue what to do at this point. I needed to get home and start putting things together. My decision needed to be mine and mine alone.

When I got home, I needed to speak with the social workers to let them know I was pregnant. They had to be told because, at 17, I was underage. They were hysterical. They ran to the phone and scheduled a doctor's appointment immediately for me to have an abortion.

Hold up...wait a minute! Did you guys even ask if I want to go for an abortion? Did you guys even think about what I wanted to do? How can you call the doctor's office and make an appointment like that? I get it. No one likes Steve. He was banned from my group home. This baby is innocent in all this drama. It's actually my baby that we are talking about. My son or daughter–my blood. This is the family I never really had! Maybe I was planning on keeping the baby.

None of the social workers cared enough to ask me what I wanted. So, "angry Ramla" came out. If you spoke to me in a harsh tone, told me what to do, threatened me, or if I felt you didn't do me right, you were getting "the other Ramla".

The next day, they dragged me to the OBGYN. My social worker was yelling at me in the hallway because I refused to go into the doctor's office. I remembered her yelling, "If you don't walk in that office, I will kick your ass!" I finally went in.

The staff kept coming into the office to calm me down. The doctor informed me of my rights about the abortion and left the paperwork for me to sign. As I looked over the papers with pen in hand, I knew at that moment I wanted to be a mother. I decided I was keeping the baby and raising him myself without the father. I would do my best to give this baby whatever it needs.

I went inside the doctor's office to tell them my decision. I walked in there with my big girl pants on and told everyone I was keeping this baby, period!

My social worker drove me back home. She never spoke to me again, even when I moved out of the group home. I know she wanted the best for me and saw a bright future for me. After I made my decision, it was time to move forward with my pregnancy and new life. The baby was on the way.

Steve was the happiest person on earth after finding out I was pregnant and that I'd decided to keep the baby. We got back together. We were trying to make this work so our baby would have a mother and father. But Steve was just born to make one mistake after the next.

CHAPTER 15
I SAW RED

It was a beautiful day. Steve took me shopping, and Alina came along with us. Steve was carrying Alina's baby girl on his chest when one of his hoes showed up. She was crying and carrying on yelling, "Why are you still with her, and what about me?"

I was like, *What??? Excuse me???* Of course, I lost it–badly. We got into a huge argument and broke out into a fight. Steve and I were fighting each other, and Alina was trying to help me. We rolled down the escalator. Alina wasn't strong enough to pull Steve away from me, and none of the people who were standing around watching chose to help.

Steve couldn't speak; all he saw was red. I was trying to break up with him for good, but I heard him smacking this girl around. Then he started running after me, but I yelled, "Get away from me!" "Get away from me!" He continued to follow me, which started another big fight. We fought down the escalator, through the entire store, and out into the street. The police showed up. They asked if I needed any help. I chose to give Steve a pass instead of diming him out and him having to return to jail. I had our child to think about. I told the police that everything was ok, then the cops left.

People on the streets were scared to get involved. Steve offered Alina a ride home with her baby. I didn't want it to sit in the passenger seat, so I sat in the backseat with Alina and her baby. He took off, and Alina and I realized he was not on his way to her house. He was on the Autobahn to another state.

He took us to a place where there was absolutely no one. It was a big field, an area where if you wanted you could kill somebody and dump the body. There was nothing. No houses, people, stores, not even a single car was driving by. Absolutely nothing.

He got out of the car and opened the door on my side. Then he dragged me out by my hair to this open field and proceeded to beat on me. Mind you, I was a couple of months pregnant. *Why is he doing this? Did he want me to lose the baby? What was wrong with him?* I thought.

Alina was trying to start the car, so I could jump in and leave his ass in that field. It didn't work because Alina wasn't good at driving a car. The engine kept dying on us, so there went that plan. We were trapped and stuck with him until he took us home. We suffered for hours until he finally calmed down. I felt so bad for Alina's daughter. She wasn't a year old yet and needed her milk and diaper changed. She was just as lost as Alina and I were.

After a while, his coke wore off, and he came back to earth. That's when he took us home. He cried and begged me to forgive him. At that point, all that B.S. was not moving me anymore. All I thought was how full of shit he was. And from that day on, I plotted to come up with a master plan to leave his ass for good. I just needed to wait for the right timing.

I fell mentally into a deep hole. I thought I would never get out of it, but I needed to get my shit together. I had to be there for my baby boy. I didn't want my baby to feel any negativity. Not while he was inside me or at any time ever.

It was 6 a.m., and Steve and I were sleeping. I woke to find my pajama bottoms were completely wet. My side of the bed was totally soaked. At first, I thought I'd peed on myself. I jumped up and ran to the kitchen. As I was running, something was pouring down my legs. I realized it was clear, which meant the baby was coming. I screamed at Steve to get out of the bed because my water had broken. He jumped up, got the car, and drove me to the hospital.

They tried to induce my labor, but I was so scared that nothing opened up down there. My baby's heartbeat stopped, and I saw doctors running to take me to the operation room immediately.

I asked what was happening, and the nurse said they needed me to sign a consent form to perform an emergency C-section right then. I threw up from all that was going on. I signed the paperwork. Then I remembered a mask being placed over my face, and that was it. March 29th, 1996 Jordan was born. My son. My baby. The person who would keep me on the right path from now on. My family.

We had a happy time, and Steve actually tried really hard to do a good job. He helped by feeding the baby, cleaning, cooking, etc.

I was ready to pack my stuff for my trade school graduation trip to Barcelona, Spain. Steve promised that he would take care of him. I wasn't sure about that, so I'd arranged for Jordan's godmother to come to watch him. Steve got so mad he started screaming he was the father, and he could do it. OK, I chose to trust him. *What can happen? He's the father, right?*

I stayed in Barcelona for ten days. I couldn't wait to get back home. Our son was six months old, and he was my heart, soul, my sunshine, my absolute everything. The next day, Steve went to work as I cleaned the house. The house phone rang. I answered the phone, and it was a girl named Yvette. She told me that she'd watched my son while I was in Barcelona and that Steve was in Amsterdam the entire time.

I was thinking, *Who are you? Why did you watch my son? Why not him? What is happening?* This woman was a stranger to me and had been watching over my son. She told me that she would rather tell me herself before I heard it from somebody else. Also, she knew about my reputation and didn't want me to find her to beat her up.

First of all, I was mad that she told me she was the one watching my son. I made a mental note to fuck her up one day. Just like I did that girl in the retail store while I was shopping with Steve and Alina.

No one was safe at that time, and I didn't care if I was a new mother or not. If you hurt me, that was it. It took me years to learn revenge was not going to heal me. Leave everything up to God and watch karma work. That's me now, but back then, I was a savage.

I hung up the phone, and my blood was boiling. I heard the door open as Steve came in.

I asked him, "Who is Yvette? Why did she watch my son while I was in Barcelona?" I popped one question after the next until he smacked me straight in my face. I saw BLACK, then NOTHING. It was so dark. I thought I went blind.

It took a minute or two for my brain to come together after that smack. My vision eventually returned, and I saw a large knife on the kitchen table. I grabbed it, and all I wanted to do was stab that fucker. *I'm done with people putting their hands on me. If he dies, so be it.* I was ready to murder him.

Steve reacted fast and grabbed Jordan. He thought that would stop me, but I saw him and only him. I was in attack mode. He quickly ran to the bedroom with the baby. He tried to close the door, and that's when I stabbed him right in the middle of his hand. I can still remember how the white wall splattered with his blood. The mint-colored carpet was full of blood. He was screaming in pain, but I couldn't care less.

After I saw the blood, I threw the knife on the floor. Steve ran to the bathroom, holding his hand over the tub. He'd lost so much blood, but I honestly enjoyed it. I felt so satisfied that he was the one in pain this time. Now he knew how I felt all those times he hurt me!

He had the nerve to ask me if I could call an ambulance for him. Do you know what I did? I dressed my baby, put him in his stroller, and took him for a walk. I left Steve to die.

An hour later, he called me to come to get him from the emergency room. I drove to pick him up. The doctors asked how he fell and injured himself on the electric fence. I told them I had no clue.

When we left the hospital, I asked him why he didn't rat me out. He said that he was from the streets and that's not what we do. He'd rather protect me than hand me to the law. I was grateful.

All I knew was, he never put his hands on me again after that day. Even if I was in his face, he controlled himself and walked away. I was still working on my master plan to get rid of him. But I was clueless about how to accomplish it. The police were not an option. Even if they locked him up, he never stayed in jail long enough. His mother was no help. He didn't listen to anyone. All those therapy sessions went out the window because he never took them seriously.

CHAPTER 16
PERFECT TIMING

Alina had her circle of friends, just a couple of people that I never wanted to hang out with. I was not close to them. Their vibes never matched mine.

One day, one of Alina's homeboys from her other set of friends started to hang out with us. His name was Jimmy, and he was from Berlin, Germany. On the Autobahn, it's about a three-hour drive. He was in town, and since I was ok with him coming out with us that night, we went to club SKYY. Jimmy was very polite and respectful, and I thought it would be good to have him with us in case Steve popped up. To everyone else, he would look like a bodyguard.

It was a Friday night, and we'd all had a good time at SKYY. We'd left the nightclub and walked to my car. Jimmy sat in the front passenger seat, I was driving, and Alina jumped in the back. She was wasted and ended up laying down in the back seat. I was tired and ready to drop them off. As I drove off, we passed Steve and his entourage. To him and his friends, it looked like I was leaving with some dude in my car. No one could see Alina in the back seat.

Just so you know, it's about to get crazy again.

As I was driving, everyone was quiet. They were dozing off, so I turned the radio on. I looked to check on Alina. She was knocked out and snoring. Her friend was snoring even louder, and it was a live concert between them. I was just driving, staying focused on the road.

When I looked in my rearview mirror, I saw the silhouette of a car behind me. I thought, *Why is this person driving without their headlights on?* Mind you, it was pitch dark outside. I told myself right away, *If this is Steve behind me, I have to find a way to shake him. I'll make random turns, and if this car is still behind me, then I know without a doubt it's Steve.* I made many random turns over and over, but he stayed right on me.

"Alina! Jimmy! Wake up. Steve is following us." Alina was sober in one second. She sat straight up, her eyes wide open. She knew Steve was not to be played with. Unfortunately, Jimmy still had no clue what was going on or what was about to happen.

I started to speed up. I began to run red lights. Thank God it was in the middle of the night, and the streets were empty. Otherwise, someone would have gotten hurt. It was winter, and snow was everywhere on the roads. It was dangerous and super slippery, but it was a risk I was willing to take because I wasn't ready to face Steve.

He caught up to me soon because he was a much better driver than I was. His car was right next to mine. He cut me off and hit my car so hard that I had to stop the vehicle. He came walking in our direction with a gun in his hand. He started to hit my windshield with the gun again and again until it completely shattered.

I got out of the car, ready for the confrontation. Surprisingly, Steve was not focused on me at all. He didn't want me. He wanted Jimmy. Steve and his boys were completely focused on this innocent kid who was sitting in the passenger seat. I started praying for him. Alina had also gotten out of the car by that time and was begging Steve and his friends to leave her homeboy alone.

I started to run for help. When I looked back, I saw Alina's boy running soooo fast! I mean, like Speedy Gonzales fast, with no shoes on! I guess he lost his shoes while they were jumping him. He was running in the ice-cold snow. I kept running. Unfortunately, I ran in the opposite direction down a dead-end street with no one in sight. Then I saw two houses. I knocked and banged on the door of the first one. No one opened the door. The second house had their lights on, so I thought someone must be home. It was 5 a.m. Everyone is home at 5 a.m., right? Nobody answered the door at the second house either. No one wanted to help. No one ever wants to get involved. *WHY????*

As a result of all those things that happened to me, I always told myself that if I saw someone on the street in danger, no matter if I'm by myself or not, no matter where I am, I would make sure I helped that person. Even if I had to dial 911 for help, I'd never ignore the situation and keep moving. PLEASE DON'T JUST SIT THERE AND DO NOTHING WHEN SOMEONE NEEDS HELP.

I screamed for them to please open the door because we needed help. Then I heard a voice asking, "Can we help you? Do you need help?" I turned around, and I saw a white car. The window was down with two men inside. They asked me again, "Do you need help? We are undercover cops." I was like, *OMG, I love you, GOD! Thank you for always sending me an angel to help and to protect me.*

I answered, "YES, PLEASE!" I pointed to Steve and his entourage. I didn't even think to tell the cops to check Steve, because he had a gun or two and probably lots of cocaine inside his car and in his bloodstream. All I wanted was for him to be behind bars. *Take him far away from me. Just arrest him already! PLEASE!!!*

I was so over it. They put the handcuffs on him. Steve looked into my eyes in disbelief when I screamed at the cops that he had weapons and drugs in the car. They found everything I told them about everything. All of the stuff in his car, on him, and they found even more illegal objects.

Meanwhile, more police arrived. While they walked everyone from his crew to police cars, I waved goodbye with a big smile on my face. Those two undercover cops with invisible angel's wings took the devil away from me. I knew they were angels because those two undercover cops came completely out of nowhere. It was the perfect time for them to arrive.

I looked at my car. It was totally destroyed. Alina was losing it. I tried to calm her down, poor girl. I felt like she had been through a lot, just being my best friend. We took a taxi home. I left my car there. Honestly, to this day, I never went back to pick up my car. I can't even tell you what happened to it.

I contacted the German Red Cross organization, and they started to help me right away. It didn't take them a week to find and move me into another apartment in a different top-secret neighborhood. I was not allowed to tell anyone where I lived. I also had a protection order against Steve.

I packed my son's belongings, a few other things, and left. I couldn't believe I was running away again! Flashbacks ran through my mind from when I ran away from home. The same scary feelings I felt then returned. Hopefully, this time I was protected once and for all from Steve.

2 Months later

The streets were talking, saying Steve was already back out. *Wow. What does it take to keep him behind bars forever? Is there anything someone can do to keep him away from me for at least a few years? He was out after two months???* I couldn't believe it. Of course, he found out where I'd moved and came to my house. *Can someone answer a question for me? How come all these crazy abusers find their victims right away like it's nothing?*

Steve's mother called me talking about how he was my son's father and all that noise. She suggested that he and I try to make our relationship work (againnnnnn) because she was sure this time it would work out.

Wait.

Give me a minute to laugh.

HA HA HA!!!!!!

But I thought, *What did I have to lose? He didn't care about the order of protection, and even when I went to the police again, they didn't do anything about it. It's like this guy is glued to me, so let's try again.*

Yay. I'm so excited.

CHAPTER 17
ALEX

Steve started a new job at a coffee shop in the Red Light District. Just for the people who do not know what a coffee shop is, back then, a coffee shop in Germany was the same as a coffee shop in Amsterdam.

You go in, and you can order and smoke weed, coke whatever drug you want. The only difference was, the ones in Amsterdam were legal, but the ones in Germany were illegal.

Alex used to be one of the big-time drug dealers in Germany. It was not easy to reach him. He was like a superstar. Steve wanted to follow in his footsteps. Steve was able to make lots of money because of Alex. He was obsessed with him. All he talked about was his boss, Alex. Alex here, Alex there, how smart and good-looking Alex was. *Oh my God, can you stop talking about this guy?* But Steve was in his happy place, making a lot of money.

I remember one night, Steve called me to pick him up, and I said no problem. Before I hung up the phone, he told me not to come inside, just wait in the car for him.

"Why?"

"I do not ever want you to meet Alex," he said.

That was so weird to me. It sounded wrong. Now, if you know me, you know that if someone tells me not to do something, it will drive me insane, and I will do the opposite.

When he said that to me, so many thoughts flooded my mind. It took about 30 minutes to drive where he was in the Red Light District. I had 30 minutes to think about why he did not want me inside that coffee shop. Maybe it was another girl or something.

I parked my car but didn't tell him that I was there. Whatever was inside that shop, I would be able to see it with my own eyes. The door was open, so I walked in. It had dim lighting, and lounge music was playing in the background. It was a beautiful bar. I was standing there, and the smell of marijuana hit my face. I was trying to locate Steve, but he was nowhere to be found.

When I turned around, I saw him standing there, talking to his business partner. I felt hot, dizzy, and my heartbeat started to pound faster and faster. It wasn't Steve that I saw; it was Alex. He was so handsome, almost perfect, picture-perfect, my type and beyond. He had beautiful long, curly hair in a ponytail. He was a handsome man, half black and half white, dressed from head to toe in Versace. *Now I understand why Steve said not to come inside.* I instantly fell in love with Alex.

Steve came out of the backroom and saw me staring at Alex. It was like his face and body language said it was too late. He took my hand and pulled me outside. Alex didn't even have the chance to notice me that night. Steve grabbed me and got me out of there as soon as possible. He literally threw me into the car, and we drove off. He was mad.

"I told you not to go in."

"How come?" I asked him again.

"Because I knew you would like Alex, and he will like you too. I would lose you one day. That's why. I never want to lose you, Ramla. You are the only one I ever loved and the only one I will ever love." I just ignored it.

Driving back home, we were both quiet. I was thinking about Alex. *What the fuck? How did Steve know my feelings would go off like that? I needed to get him out of my mind because obviously, I'm driving home with Steve, not with Alex.*

Steve started having pain in his joints and bones. He was not feeling well enough to leave the house, so he stopped working at the coffee shop. He stopped running the streets and stayed home a lot. He told me he would watch the baby and I could take a break and go out with my friends.

I went to my Sunday dance practice, where I met my friend Lora. Lora was a beautiful dancer, one of our African Legacy lead dancers. She asked me if I wanted to go out that night. It was a Sunday, so I asked if it was really popping on Sundays. She laughed so hard at me, then asked if I'd ever heard about sweet Sundays at Café Keese. She told me those parties were only once a month on a Sunday, and this Sunday night was VIP only. That Sunday night was Keith Sweat's night, and singers were always flown in from the U.S. to perform there.

I told Lora I was in. I called Steve and told him I wasn't coming home after practice and was going out to a house club. He laughed at me because he thought all he ever had to worry about were the dudes at the hip-hop club, not a gay house club. But that was the night he lost me for good.

Everything changed in one second. My master plan was on. Everything felt so right that night. The entire atmosphere, the universe, everything was on my side. The time had come for me to taste freedom. The time was tonight.

Lora was right. It was a gay scene. Drag queens greeted us with shots at the door. The music was so good all night long. I fell in love with house music that night. The club was packed with unique, beautiful people. Dancers from London were flown in to go-go dance on the main stage. I could go on and on about that night. It was the most epic night I ever had.

Lora turned around and looked at me like she'd seen a ghost.

"What?" I asked.

"Do you know who I just saw?"

"No."

"It's Alex. He is right there in that section." As soon as she said that, we saw him walking in our direction.

Lora knew him. He grabbed her hand and kissed it—his way of saying hello. I also did not realize Lora was into him, but I could not blame her. He was so fine. She told me that he was dating an Arabic girl named Halema, who was a psycho. No one wanted to get close to Alex because of her crazy ass.

Alex didn't see me. I wondered if I was invisible. I mean, he really paid me no mind at all. But then I remembered that Steve was his boy, and maybe he was ignoring me out of respect. My heart was beating fast again, but I couldn't say anything because Lora was just as crazy about him as I was. So why say anything and hurt her feelings? I enjoyed myself that night.

It was almost 8 a.m., and the club was about to turn their lights on. I was sitting on the stairs next to the DJ, by the stage. I lost Lora, as we were both tipsy.

I was just sitting there watching everyone. It was like a movie. The club was already getting empty.

Then I felt someone sitting close next to me, really close. So close that I felt the breath on my neck. I turned around, and it was Alex. I didn't say a word as he came even closer to me and asked me if I was Ramla. I said, yes. He asked me if I was the one that Steve beats up. I said, yes. Alex looked away and shook his head.

He looked down and asked, "How can a man beat up a woman. I feel sorry for him. You are so beautiful. Now I know why he is hiding you from the world. You don't deserve to be in a relationship like that. He should never put his hands on you again." Then he whispered in my ear, "I wish the baby you had was mine." He got up and walked away.

Oh my God, are you kidding me? He did not just say that and walk away! That means the entire time I thought I was invisible to him, I actually wasn't! I was on his mind. He knew about me and wants me. Let the game begin.

I was tipsy, and I didn't care about Alex much right then because I needed to use the bathroom and look for Lora. *How the hell am I supposed to go home?* The restroom was in the basement, and there were couches down there. It was very classy for a bathroom.

I walked out of the bathroom, and Alex was standing there, waiting for me.

"I'm looking for Lora," I said to him.

"I know. She's upstairs waiting for us."

"Us?"

"Yes, we are all going to have breakfast together, then I'll drive you guys home."

So it was Alex, his friend, Lora and me. We drove to a restaurant nearby. It was a luxury restaurant. Only people with big names were able to get a table there. As soon as we arrived, they treated us like royalty because of Alex. Alex was the man. The more I saw that, the more I wanted him.

Lora and I were starving. It was actually a good idea to grab something to eat before we went home. We could not believe we were going to eat with Alex. I wanted to pinch myself to see if I was dreaming.

After we finished our breakfast, we walked back to the car. I felt him staring at me, but I acted like I didn't notice it. At the time, I was really shy. We got to his car, which I didn't notice earlier because I was drunk, but now that I'd sobered up, I couldn't believe the car we were in.

He probably had the best car in town. He was loaded with money, and you could tell that he did not care because he was friendly and humble.

He dropped off his friend first, then Lora. He had a plan. I was in the back seat, snoring. I was knocked out. When I opened my eyes, I saw Alex, looking at me in his rearview mirror. I jumped up and realized I didn't know where I was. I looked out of the window and saw we were on the Autobahn. The sun was bright, he had the radio on, and we were listening to relaxing house music.

"Good morning, beautiful. I was watching you sleep the entire time. You are so beautiful." I was still in shock. I didn't know if I was still asleep because it felt like I was in a movie!

He passed me his cell phone and said, "Call your babysitter right now and tell her to watch your son until next weekend."

What??? Oh my god!!! I started thinking about the scenario, and everyone involved and started shaking and panicking. *My son! Steve! I'm here with Alex, Steve's boss! I am dead.*

"Turn around. I can't do this. I have a son. I'm still living with Steve, and he will kill me. Also, what about your crazy girlfriend?" I asked.

"Relax. I broke up with her, so you don't have to worry about anything. There won't be any drama for you ever."

I called Nena, one of my best friends, who was also my son's godmother. I told her where I was and who I was with, and she almost choked on her drink. She could not believe that I was with Alex. She was so happy for me and said not to worry and that she would take care of Jordan. I told her to make sure she did not leave my baby with Steve since I had zero trust in him. After what happened when I went to Barcelona, Steve knew better than to fuck with me again! When it comes to my son, I'm the only one who makes the decisions.

After Nena gave me the ok, I knew my baby was in good hands. I stopped shaking and calmed down. I just wanted to enjoy myself. I couldn't remember the last time I felt this happy, other than when I gave birth to my son.

I looked next to me and saw a huge life-size teddy bear. That teddy bear was actually bigger than me! It was a teddy bear that I always wanted and never got from my parents because they couldn't afford it. My first reaction was to jump on that bear and give him a huge hug.

"Where did the teddy bear come from?"

"I stopped at the store while you were sleeping and bought it for you. It's yours."

Right then and there, I thought there must be a catch with this guy.

He can't be that perfect.

CHAPTER 18
AMSTERDAM

I was still in the back when he told me to jump in the passenger seat. I went up front to sit next to him. He took my hand and kissed it. It was just Alex and me. I asked him where he was taking me, and he said that we would arrive in Amsterdam in a few minutes.

He took me to Holland, my favorite town in Amsterdam. We checked into a beautiful luxury five-star hotel, right in the heart of Central Station.

I fell so deeply in love with him that nothing in the world mattered anymore. The only thing I wanted in life was someone who loved me. Someone who really noticed and understood who I was. But the most important thing to me was to be with someone who could protect me from the evil that seemed to keep finding me.

I felt safe with Alex. No one could do anything bad to me anymore with him by my side. If a person tried to hurt me, Alex was right there to take care of it the same day.

Once I was ready, we left the hotel. He took me on a shopping spree and got me everything that looked good on me. He didn't buy a thing for himself. He bought me clothes and shoes and also bought some clothes for my son. I did not ask for any of that. He walked into the sneaker store and asked me for Jordan's shoe size. When the sales associate came out with beautiful expensive sneakers, I was blown away.

Mind you, I grew up poor. There was no luxury of any kind in my life.

Everything Alex did that day was special to me. The most special thing was that he thought of my son. Jordan was my everything. Alex was ready to be in his life, and he started to show me. A woman can recognize when a man appreciates her. I could tell at that moment that this man was in love with me.

A week passed by, and we were on our way back to Germany. Back then, my cell phone service was working in Germany only, so my phone was out of service while we were away. Alex gave me his phone to call the babysitter. He had an international service plan, which at that time, only rich people could afford. He connected my number to his cell phone line on our way back to Germany. That meant if someone called my phone, it went straight to his phone.

After setting up my number, his phone started to ring immediately. It was Steve. I started shaking all over.

Alex said, "Don't worry." He held my hands. "You don't need to talk to or deal with him ever again. I am here for you and Jordan. You're mine now. I know everyone is scared of him but look into my eyes right now. Do you know who I am? Do you know what I do? If you don't know, ask the streets. I am Alex, and I am not scared of him. I got you, and I will protect you. He will never put his hands on you again."

Listening to Alex's words put me at ease. For the first time in a long time, I felt safe. His voice calmed me down. This whole situation with Alex and Steve felt like someone was punching me in the stomach.

You know when people say they have butterflies in their stomach? Usually, it comes from a happy place. When I say I feel something in my stomach, it usually comes from a negative place. I never called them butterflies in my stomach, because my pain was real. I felt my father's punch in my stomach. I called them "Killer Flies" because each punch felt like I would die.

The phone didn't stop ringing. Steve was very persistent. After Alex calmed me down, he picked up the phone and said hello. It was quiet for a second.

Steve said, "Please don't tell me this is YOU with her right now."

Alex said, "Yes, it's me, and what are you going to do about it? NOTHING! She's mine, and your son is mine. That's my family now, and you will leave her alone forever. You had your chance with her multiple times, years, and you blew it. She is not your punching bag. She is my girl now."

I never saw anyone stand up for me like that, when it came to Steve. I wished Alex had been in my life to defend me from my father and Blondy all those years ago.

This man was more accomplished than Steve, and that was exactly what I needed to end our relationship. My master plan was working. He told Steve to meet up with him as soon as we got back to Germany, which was an hour away.

Steve better be ready, I thought.

CHAPTER 19
HAPPY PLACE

When we got back to Hamburg, Alex wanted me to drop him off where he was supposed to meet Steve, then take his car and leave. He didn't want me to be there. No one knew what was going to happen, so he wanted to keep me safe. He told me that he would call me after. I was scared. I knew both of them carried guns, so I prayed the whole ride that everything would go smoothly.

As soon as I dropped off Alex, I was on my way to pick up Jordan. I wasn't on the road five minutes before Alex called and told me to turn around and get him. *That was fast! That talk was way too quick. Something is wrong.* As I drove back, I saw Alex standing outside their second coffee shop, waiting for me with a bunch of other people.

He jumped in the car and said, "It's done. Let's go."

My heart was beating fast again. That punch in my stomach, that "Killer Flies" feeling, came back.

I asked him, "What did Steve say? What happened?"

"As soon as I saw Steve, I told him that you were my girl now, right in front of his face, and Steve passed out. They have him in the back room now, taking care of him. He'll be fine. Let's get your son and go home."

Home? "Home" was at that time with Steve. Where is my home now? I thought.

Alex continued, "Steve is not coming back to your house. You have to move out of your apartment as soon as possible. You can move in with me, or we can get a new place of our own together."

Steve tried only one time to get back at Alex. I remember we were sleeping, and Alex's phone was ringing. Steve was telling him to come downstairs. Alex jumped up, grabbed his gun, and ran downstairs. I put my fingers deep inside my ears and started to sing, like a little girl in one of those horror movies. I didn't want to hear any gunshots, and I didn't want anyone to die.

As much as Steve hurt me, I knew he loved me. He didn't know any other way. He was still my son's father, and he used to be my best friend. Now I was blaming myself. *I was so stupid to get involved with crazy Alex. This guy is way too gangster. He will kill Steve!*

I looked out the window, and I saw Steve lying on Alex's car, with all his people. Alex went straight up and punched him in the face. He didn't stop hitting him. It almost felt like that time my father beat up Blondy in the hallway. Steve gave up, and the fight was finally over. Thank God. No one used their guns, and no one got hurt.

That was the last time I ever heard from Steve. He respected my relationship with Alex and left me alone. I only saw him when he came to pick up or drop off Jordan. He also brought over clothes for Jordan. He was nice, but oh well, who cares at this point, it's over now. Steve and I tried to go back to just being friends again. I should have kept it that way anyway, but you live and learn.

Alex and I found a nice apartment in the city and moved in together. We were such a cute family, and Jordan loved him. There was so much peace and love in the house.

All my other friends were so truly grateful to finally see me happy. Alex and I were like Romeo and Juliet, a dream couple. No one could come between us. Jordan saw him as his dad, and Alex took every opportunity to spend time with him. I was in such a happy place for the FIRST time in my life.

There was not a day where Alex didn't spoil me. Every morning he left me a stack of money on the kitchen table. Whenever he went shopping for himself, he always thought of me and came back home with a beautiful dress or some other incredible gift for me. I told him to stop buying me expensive stuff. I was never really into designer brands, but his answer was he was into it. I didn't feel ok when he bought something for me and not himself too.

Whatever I did, he was a part of me every single day.

CHAPTER 20
DON'T OPEN THE DOOR

I loved Alex so much. Even today, there is not one bad thing I can say about him. He was an angel sent at the right time and the right place. He was sent to save me and make me and Jordan happy.

I remember the day I picked up Jordan from daycare, and Alex was still on the streets. I was cleaning up when someone was knocking on my door. I walked to the door and asked who was there. No answer. I asked again, and again, and again. I looked through the peephole. I couldn't see a thing, so I opened the door and saw a disturbed looking girl standing there, looking at me.

She had her hands in her pockets, and I was getting a bad feeling in my stomach. Jordan ran to the door and stood next to me while holding my legs.

"Hey," he said to her.

When I think about that moment and the look on her face when she saw Jordan, it was then that she decided to change her plan. I just know it.

My brain clicked right away, and I put two and two together. I knew this was Alex's ex, or who knows, maybe still his girl. Whatever she was, I needed to think fast because I had a feeling she had a knife in her pocket, and she was ready to kill Alex, Jordan, or me. She probably would have killed anyone of us. My son was there, and I needed to think fast.

She asked me, "Is Alex inside?"

"No, he is not here right now." I asked, "Do you want to come in and wait for him? Do you want a cup of tea or something to drink?" It just felt right at that moment to calm her down and make her feel like I was on her side.

She walked into my house and went straight to the kitchen. I told her to have a seat and calm down. I made her a cup of tea.

"Let's talk," I said.

"Alex is the love of my life, and if I can't have him, then no one can. People told me about you and how he is so in love with you."

She started crying. She could not believe he started dating a girl with a toddler when he'd told her to abort the child they'd made together. How could he tell her to get rid of their baby, but wanted to date another girl who had a baby? That right there messed with her mind.

The more she talked about Alex, the more she started to mess up the perfect picture that I had of him. As she was shaking and sitting at the kitchen table, she reached into her coat pocket and pulled out a knife. My intuition I had earlier was correct. I moved her cup of tea toward her, and at the same time, slowly took the knife away from her. I told her it wasn't worth going to jail. If she really wanted him back, she could have him.

All I'm thinking about is Jordan. SHIT! How can I get her out of here?

She wouldn't stop crying, so I decided to call Alex. I told her to calm down, and I'll ask Alex to come over right now so she could talk to him in peace. His phone rang, and I made sure I didn't take my eyes off of her. Jordan was glued to me. I was ready for whatever at this moment. All I knew was if someone had to die, it would be her.

Alex picked up the phone.

"How far are you from my house?" I asked.

"Ten minutes."

"Please come home right now. I need you." I couldn't say more because she was right next to me.

He was there in five minutes. He felt something was wrong; maybe he heard it in my voice. When he walked in, and within seconds of seeing her sitting in my kitchen, he jumped on her and started beating her down. I didn't expect him to react that way.

I grabbed Jordan, ran to his room, locked the door, and tried to distract him. I didn't want my son to see or hear any of this. She was crying and screaming; she was in so much pain. I felt terrible for her, especially hearing her screaming because a man is hitting her. I felt a knife in my heart. I couldn't do anything. I needed to protect my son. I just couldn't help her; Jordan was the number one priority.

A few minutes later, it was quiet. I thought maybe he dragged her out and finished her outside. So I told Jordan to be quiet, that mommy would be right back and to please not leave his room.

I opened the door slowly. There was no one in the kitchen or any of the other rooms. The front door was wide open. I saw blood everywhere. That punching belly "Killer Flies" feeling came inside me again.

Then I saw her standing there, with a bloody knife in her hand. I was so scared, and my whole body started to shake. *Oh my god! Where is Alex? Did she kill him? Why did I ask him to come over without warning him?* I was driving myself crazy with all these questions. I know something bad happened; I just didn't know exactly what. *Now maybe she will kill me or Jordan.*

I went up to her to calm her down. I took the same knife from her hand again.

"What did you do? Where is Alex? Why is there blood all over the place, and on the knife?"

She looked at me and told me after he beat her up and got up to walk out, she grabbed the knife that he bought for her one day as a gift and stabbed him in his back. He collapsed right away, but still tried to crawl out of the house. She didn't know where he went.

Now here I am with this psycho ex-girlfriend. I can't even call the police, because she's right in front of me. All I want to do is keep her happy for now, because she is a different level of crazy.

Thirty minutes went by, which felt like hours. Then my phone rang. It was Alex. I was so happy to see his name on my display! He called me from the emergency room. He knew how crazy she was, so he needed to find a way to get Jordan and me out of this situation safely.

He could barely talk, and I heard the doctors telling him to hang up because they were about to operate on him. He was seconds away from dying. This crazy girl missed his lungs by millimeters.

Before he hung up, he said, "Please come to the hospital now, and bring her with you. Tell her that I need her and that I love her." *What??? Are you kidding me??? I was like I knew it, he is not perfect, just like every other man.* "Please do what I tell you. You'll find out why later." I was like, *Fuck him, fuck her, let me take her ass to him, and I'm out.*

But Alex had a plan. All I needed to do was trust him. I put positive energy around me and started praying again. I put my faith and hope in Alex. I strapped Jordan in his car seat, asked her to get into my car, and drove to the hospital.

As much as I loved Alex, I could not imagine him having another girl. I kind of felt bad for her. I knew she was extremely hurt. I was driving and holding her hand at the same time because I felt sorry for her. It really calmed her down a lot. I knew right then and there that she was out to hurt Alex, not me.

As soon as I parked my car at the hospital, my car was surrounded by police. Lights were all over the place. They already knew that she was the one that stabbed Alex. They went straight to her and placed her in handcuffs. She was arrested on the spot. I felt safe but still sad for her at the same time.

Alex had set her up.

CHAPTER 21
INTERNATIONAL SEARCH

A year went by, drama free. Alex recovered quickly from his injuries and was back on his street game. We went out to the most beautiful places you can imagine. After what happened with his ex, Alex developed strong emotional feelings for me. Don't ask me why. I don't know. Maybe the thought of losing me made his love grow stronger.

But my feelings about him changed. *He hit a woman right in front of my eyes. He drove her crazy. And was he not the one who had talked so much shit about Steve? How could Steve put his hands on me and blah, blah, blah. Now you hit a woman, right in front of my eyes. Why? Just because she was crazy in love with you?* I no longer looked at him the same way. And when I get turned off, I'm turning into *that bitch.* I just can't help it.

One day he asked me if I wanted to go outside to smoke a cigarette with him. We were standing on the balcony at night, I looked up and saw a full moon.

"I have to ask you something. It's very important."

"What is it?"

"Will you run away with me? Of course, we will take Jordan with us. I will take care of you guys, you know I will."

I was like, *Run away? From who? What is happening here?* He said that he found out that the police put out an international search for him. He was wanted all over the country and he couldn't go anywhere. We needed to leave now before they came.

"No! Please do not tell me that. As much as I love you, I love my son more. I'm not doing this. Thank you for everything, but you are on your own. I am not a criminal. My father did not raise a criminal. I am Ramla Tarkhani! An A+ student, smart, and sometimes stupid. I'm a mother now, and I can't make unhealthy decisions anymore. I have to be a role model for my son. Jordan can't look up to his drug dealer father, or Alex the gangster, with his international search. I know I got myself into this shit. Now I have to get myself out of this situation."

I needed to stop all this RIGHT NOW. As cold-hearted as it sounds, my son was number one. That's why God sent me Jordan. He was there to keep me grounded and help me to make better decisions at the right time.

Alex went to his knees, with tears rolling down his cheeks, begging me to go with him.

"They will never find us, I have everything planned."

"No. I can't do it. You got to go now." I told him. He took all his stuff and left.

A week later, Nena and I took my son to the park. That's when I saw Alex walking in our direction. I didn't know what would happen. He grabbed me by my hair, smacked me in my face, in broad daylight at the park. He slapped me in a crowded park and then just walked away. That was the last time I ever saw him.

The police never found Alex. The streets were saying that he flew with a new identity to the Dominican Republic. When he was gone, that's when it hit me. It hit me hard. I had that "Killer Flies" feeling in my stomach again, but this time on the worst level ever. I fell into a long, deep depression.

I was never mad at Alex, even when he hit me in the park. I knew he needed to get his anger out before he left for good. I knew I'd hurt him so much by not leaving with him, but I need to do what was best for my son.

It took me eight years to get over Alex. Eight long years to get out of that dark hole. I even cut my hair, almost like what my father did to me when he cut off my hair. I cried myself to sleep each night after I put Jordan to bed for almost eight years. When I was alone, my pain was so bad. I didn't want anyone to see me like that.

I was not ready to fall in love again. Every man I met was a loser in my eyes. He'd spoiled me so much that no one could measure up. I couldn't even have sex with anyone. I was so miserable.

I graduated from college. I'd also found a boss job at one of the biggest marketing companies around. I was making a huge amount of money each week.

I'd signed a record deal with Marlboro Music with the group Double Up. Our song was playing on the radio, and our music video was on all music channels like MTV, VHI, and VIVA TV (a German music channel from back in the day). We performed everywhere in Germany. We also flew to Tokyo, Japan, for VIVA TV to host a TV show for them.

Fans started to recognize me on the streets and asked for autographs. My dreams were starting to come true! My music career began to slowly help me forget about the struggles and abuse I'd received from my father, Blondy, Steve, and Alex.

Lora had just come back from NYC. As soon as she landed, she came with Alina to check on me. She was talking all day about New York and how I would absolutely love it there. She said once I stepped on that NYC soil, I'd never want to leave. I'd feel like it was my home.

Alina was dating a new dude, Larry. He had family in New York. One day, Larry surprised Alina and bought her a plane ticket to NYC. He gave it to her on her birthday, right before Christmas Eve. Larry also bought a plane ticket for me, her BFF, considering how tight we were. When he told us about our upcoming trip to NYC, we were so happy and excited that Alina and I literally started to dance in the street!

I needed to get FAR away from Hamburg, Germany. I had to forget about all the abuse that was still messing with me mentally. It was 1999 when I flew to NYC for the first time. Just when I thought my life would be normal and peaceful again, a NEW NIGHTMARE started.

Oh, God. Why???

To be continued...

A WORD FROM THE AUTHOR

This is the first part of my story. I have to keep saying it but, I still can't believe that I have accomplished writing a book. I can say one thing after I finish the last sentence in my last chapter. I felt happy and healed. It was the BEST therapy I could ever get.

All I'm trying to say is, if you go down a rough road, pick up a pen and paper and start writing. Write as much as you can. If you feel like giving up, that's ok. Take breaks, even for years, but to fully heal, you need to get back at it and finish your story. Watch how you feel when you finish your story! It will HEAL you. Also, you should not care what this person or that person thinks about your story. If they don't like it, then oh well, it wasn't for them. It was for you, to heal—just a tip from someone who has been through hell and back.

Ramla

ABOUT THE AUTHOR

Ramla Tarkhani-Lloyd was born and raised in Hamburg, Germany. She moved to NYC in 2007 and is now based in Brooklyn, NY. Ramla is a writer and author of the new novel *I AM RAMLA*.

I AM RAMLA is her first published work. She takes her readers back in time, letting the readers feel exactly what is happening at that moment. She brings all her characters to life. Her main reason for writing this book was to heal from her abusive childhood. "It was the best therapy." "Writing this book was the beginning of my healing process."

She hopes after reading her story, it will heal those who are in an abusive relationship. Please spread her message to the world:

"You should help someone if they need your help."

Made in the USA
Middletown, DE
19 February 2020

85051971R00085